Voice of
an Angel

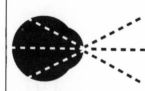

Voice of an Angel

MY LIFE (SO FAR)

Charlotte Church

Thorndike Press • Waterville, Maine

Published in 2001 by arrangement with Warner Books, Inc.

Thorndike Press Large Print Biography Series.

The tree indicium is a trademark of Thorndike Press.

The text of this Large Print edition is unabridged.
Other aspects of the book may vary from the original edition.

Set in 16 pt. Plantin by Christina S. Huff.

Printed in the United States on permanent paper.

Library of Congress Cataloging-in-Publication Data

Church, Charlotte, 1986-
    Voice of an angel : my life (so far) / Charlotte Church.
      p. cm.
   Originally published: New York : Warner Books, 2001
   ISBN 0-7862-3403-2 (lg. print : hc : alk. paper)
  1. Church, Charlotte, 1986-   2. Sopranos (Singers) —
Biography.   3. Large type books.   I. Title.
ML420.C5 A3 2001
782′.0092—dc21   2001027609
  [B]

Dedicated to everyone who has supported me:
my family, friends, and fans

Christmas

Christmas 2000. The house is filled with light and laughter. Fairy lights and happy laughter. All the family is here. My mum, my dad, my auntie Caroline (that's Mum's younger sister), my uncle Mark (that's Auntie Caroline's partner), my cousin Elliot, their son, and my grandparents Bampy and Nan. We're sitting around the table in the dining room. Normally we have Christmas Day at Bampy and Nan's house, but we've moved and our house is bigger, so this year everyone has come to us. The only real difference between their house and our house is that we've got enough dining room chairs to seat everyone — and our table is bigger. At Nan's house I always sit on the kitchen stool — and we all bump elbows.

Nan is sitting at the head, and next to her is Bampy.

Bampy's telling a story about the rock 'n' roll band he played rhythm guitar with in the sixties. The band was called the Solid Six. He's telling us about the time they toured Israel. The Israeli Prime Minister came to one of the concerts, and all the girls wanted Bampy's autograph. It's a story we've heard a million times before, but it's the way he tells it.

"It was all rock 'n' roll," he says, and we laugh.

Dad's filling everyone's glasses, and Mum's wearing the gold earrings I gave her for Christmas. They look pretty with her red hair. And here's Auntie Caroline coming in with the turkey. It's the biggest turkey you've ever seen. It's almost bigger than little Elliot. Elliot is only five, and he looks like Bart Simpson with his spiky blond hair and eager face. He's like my little brother, really.

It's good to be home.

The last few months have been so hectic. We went on an amazing trip to Hong Kong and Singapore, where I gave two concerts. The Prime Minister's wife was the guest of honor at the concert in Singapore, which made it extra special. We had a day off in Hong Kong and went on a boat trip and explored the city's bustling streets. I bought

Oriental decorations for my bedroom — and we saw the biggest statue of Buddha I've ever seen.

Then we went to Los Angeles, where I sang at a benefit gala in Hollywood called the Carousel of Hope for children with diabetes. It was held at the Beverly Hilton, and it was the most glamorous event I've ever performed at. The other singers participating were Toni Braxton and Ricky Martin. Gregory Peck was there and President Ford and Dustin Hoffman and John Travolta. Mum was so starstruck, she couldn't stop turning in her seat and whispering (very loudly), "Look, Char. Look who it is."

"Yes, Mom," I kept saying. "I can see, too."

We were both given couture dresses by L.A. designers Cantu and Castillo to wear, and even more fabulous, I was lent a ruby-and-diamond necklace by Van Cleef & Arpels that was worth $180,000. Can you imagine? I felt like Cinderella when she got to go to the ball. I couldn't believe how lucky I was. From Los Angeles we flew to Chicago and then on to Detroit. I love doing concerts in America. Everyone's so friendly.

Finally we went to Vienna, where I sang a duet with Placido Domingo for a TV special, "Christmas in Vienna." I was really looking forward to meeting him and singing together. I've always been a big fan of his, and although it can sometimes be a disappointment meeting famous people, it was fabulous to meet him. He looks like a film star, and I had goose bumps when we sang. His voice is so rich.

Both my private tutors came with me because I had so much schoolwork to get through. It was fun but exhausting.

Nan gets worried when I work too hard.

She likes it when I'm home in Cardiff, and I miss her when I'm away. I miss all my family and my friends. That's why Christmas is so special, because it's a celebration of the part of my life that's really, really important to me.

Home life.

Last night we went to midnight Mass at St. Mary's Catholic Church. St. Mary's is the local church in Canton, which is the neighborhood where Nan and Bampy and Auntie Caroline and Uncle Mark and Elliot live. It's where we used to live until we moved. St. Mary's is the church where I was christened and where I took my first Holy Communion. I always sing a carol at midnight Mass. Normally I sing "Silent Night," but this year I decided to sing "O Holy

Night." It's a Catholic carol and a favorite of mine.

My family is Catholic. And although I don't get to church very often because I'm traveling so much, I never miss midnight Mass on Christmas Eve. It's so atmospheric. There is the excitement of knowing that the next day is Christmas Day, and there's a feeling of peacefulness.

The priest at St. Mary's is called Father Delaney. He's in his seventies and looks like Gene Wilder. He's very tall, with unruly black hair. He's known me since I was a baby. He christened me, and he took my first Holy Communion, so I suppose, in a way, he's like my figurehead of faith. He has a great sense of humor. He isn't one of these priests who says you have to believe this and you mustn't believe that. I once asked him to explain sin, and he said if you feel guilty, then you've committed a sin. He says to try to live as best a life you can. To try to be a good person. That's his motto.

I think it's a good one.

In his sermon he talked about looking back at the year. Since most of the time I don't have a second to think about what I'm doing, Christmas is one time when I can reflect on the life I'm leading. I know Mum thanks God for the life we're leading. She

11

thinks of my singing as a gift from God.

She thinks I'm blessed.

I pray, too, but in my own way. Prayer is private, and for me being in church isn't about being Catholic, it's about having some sort of faith.

All I can say is, I believe in something.

Saying good-bye to 2000 and hello to 2001 symbolized so many things.

So much happened last year. What I was really looking forward to was being able to live a bit more like a normal fifteen-year-old — and I have. What I've really enjoyed this year is waking up in my own bed in the mornings. Seeing my friends. Going to parties. Going to school. I have to do my GCSEs (examinations you need to pass to get into high school) in a year's time, so right now it's important to concentrate on my studies.

And for the first time in three years I'm not recording an album this year. It's mostly so that I can go to school, but also, to be honest, because I don't know what direction I'm going to take my voice next. This year is important for experimenting to see what sounds I can make. It's giving me space.

But I'm getting away from my story.

Elliot was the first to wake up this morning. When he raced downstairs in his pajamas to open his stocking, which Santa

12

Claus had left by the mantelpiece in the living room, it wasn't even seven o'clock. We heard him shrieking with excitement. I gave him lots of Pokémon toys that I bought in Hong Kong. He loves Pokémon. Mum bought him a pair of cowboy boots with real spurs from Los Angeles. He wants to be a cowboy when he grows up.

The great thing about being in the new house is that it's big enough to sleep all the family. There are six bedrooms. The other day Mum told me how proud she is that her fourteen-year-old daughter can buy her own dream home.

"It's amazing," she said.

I suppose it is.

What's really amazing is my bedroom, which is soundproofed so that I can have all my friends sleep over and we can play music really loud and Mum and Dad can't hear us. Though I have to say the swimming pool is amazing.

And you should see our Christmas tree.

It's in the entrance hall, and it's seven feet tall and covered with decorations from all over the world. Glass snowflakes from New York. An old-fashioned Santa Claus that I found in a Christmas decoration shop in Milwaukee. He has a tartan coat and a big beard and a staff made of twigs. Then there are the red dragons that I found in Hong Kong and hundreds of white lights that sparkle like diamonds. Sitting on top of the tree is an angel wearing a glittery dress and a silver halo.

Underneath the tree are everyone's gifts wrapped in pink and blue and gold.

I love giving presents to my family.

I love watching their expressions as they open their gifts.

For Auntie Caroline, I bought a big bottle of her favorite perfume, Knowing, by Estée Lauder. I bought Nan photo frames because she has photos of all the family all over her house. I bought Bampy a book of photographs of famous fifties rock 'n' rollers, and I bought Dad a load of CDs. I have to keep him up-to-date with music; otherwise he'd be in the dark ages. Well, stuck in the eighties, anyway.

I usually get the same kinds of things. I always get lots of makeup because everyone who knows me knows that I can never have enough lip gloss and eye shadow and mascara. I love makeup. And I always get about eighty pairs of pajamas as well as books and CDs and jewelry. Last year Mum gave me a diamond solitaire ring, which I wear on special occasions. I love it. This year I asked for a pair of earrings to match.

Mum has put my new CD, Dream a Dream, on the stereo in the living room. Normally I hate listening to my own music, but it's a Christmas album of Christmas songs, so I suppose it's allowed. We all like listening to Christmas carols on Christmas Day.

Last night on TV we watched the Christmas special *Charlotte at Christmas in the Holy Land*, which I made in Jerusalem in the summer. I felt funny watching myself on TV, but it was amazing to see the Holy Land again. I felt overwhelmed by everything when I was there. Not only was it unbelievably hot (it was at least one hundred degrees), but everywhere you went, you were confronted by history. There was so much to learn.

Mum came to Jerusalem, too.

Mum always says a prayer before getting on a plane. Actually, she says three prayers. She says one for the family, one for a safe journey, and one to ask God that if he's going to take us, could he take us all together. Never in her wildest dreams did she think she would get the chance to visit the sites where Jesus walked, where he was crucified, and where his body was laid.

I learned so many interesting facts when I was there.

For example, the number of kings who went to Bethlehem was probably fifty, not three. It could have taken Mary and Joseph six months to get to Bethlehem. They might have been in Bethlehem for days or months before Jesus was born. When Jesus was born, Mary was only fourteen years old.

Sometimes I think my head is older than it should be. Sometimes when I'm traveling and missing everyone at home, I think how much I want to be normal and have a normal life and normal problems, although I guess everyone's problems seem normal to them, however big or small they are. Mum says that if I've had enough of working, I should give it up.

But I don't want to give it up.

I love singing. I love traveling, and what I love most of all is learning. Learning about other people's lives gives you a perspective on your own life. It gives you inspiration — which is something I also get from my family.

I wouldn't be where I am today, singing around the world and meeting famous people, if it wasn't for the love and encouragement of my family at home. Music is a gift in my family, and I know that I have a special gift. Mum always says she knew I'd succeed as a performer, just not this early on. My family always said that I had "it." That thing you can't define — whatever it takes. It's my family who have given me the confidence to perform — and succeed.

Which reminds me.

Tomorrow is Boxing Day, the day when all the family — all my mum's cousins and their kids, my second cousins — get together for a huge singsong. We all go to the Culver House Cross, which is a pub owned by Mum's cousin. Everyone does a turn. Cousin Paul thinks he's Elvis. He'll be singing "Jailhouse Rock" and "Love Me Tender" and "Glory, Glory, Hallelujah" as his grand finale.

"Elvis has now left the building," he says as he leaves the stage.

Auntie Caroline is a cabaret singer. She will do a song from her set. Maybe Madonna's disco version of "Don't Cry for Me, Argentina." Cousin Linda and her husband, Derek, might sing a Luther Vandross song or a thirties love song. Linda's daughter, Nadine, will sing a Whitney Houston song, and Jenna, that's Paul's daughter, always sings "My Heart Will Go On." You know — the song from *Titanic*.

What do I sing?

Generally I don't. It's my day off. The family tease me. Go on, they say, but they also understand that I want to relax. The family treats me like a normal fourteen-year-old who happens to have a job that takes her away a lot. They're not that impressed.

But my family have supported me writing this book.

They understand why I'm writing a book when I'm only fourteen. They know, like I do, that I've still got a lot of growing up to do. I've still got a lot of learning to do. But at the same time, they can see how my story might be interesting to other people.

The thing is, in the past few years I've done things people can only dream of.

I've done things people never do in a lifetime.

I've sung for the President of the United States of America. I've sung for the Queen and for the Pope. Before Christmas I went back to Washington, D.C., to switch on the lights on the White House Christmas tree. I was so thrilled to meet President Clinton again. I think he's a great guy. I've also been involved in a major legal suit with an ex-manager, and I've raised money for charity.

But my family understand that fame isn't a big deal.

They understand that fame is just a word.

Being famous is no different from being normal.

I think famous people consider them-selves normal. I know I do. If you surround yourself with normal people — like Mum and Dad and Auntie Caroline and Nan and Bampy and all my other aunties and uncles and cousins — who tell you when you're wrong or being a pain, then you're going to be normal.

I do all the regular things teenagers do, like have sleep-overs with my friends.

We gossip about boys and clothes and music, and I can forget about the person I have to be when I'm in public and I have to smile and be nice and talk to journalists and answer questions and shake hands.

I can be myself.

I can even be in a bad mood.

Because at the end of the day I'm just a fourteen-year-old girl trying to work out what it all means.

I know I'm very lucky.

This is my story.

Voice of an Angel

1

I'm Born (Phew!)

I suppose if we're going to start at the beginning, we should start right at the beginning with the stuff I can't remember. Like my birth.

To be honest, the story of my birth is a bit traumatic and definitely not much fun, so I'm going to pass you over to my mum, whose name, by the way, is Maria. She can give you all the gory details.

And just so you've got the full picture, we're at home right now. We're sitting on the yellow leather couch in our living room, and we're drinking tea. In my house, the kettle is *always* on, and someone is always asking, "Who wants a cup of tea?" And it's usually my dad, whose name is James.

Dad makes a wicked cup of tea.

Anyway, Mum's trying to look serious, but it never lasts long. A smile is twitching at the corner of her mouth. She's screwing up her chocolate brown eyes, and now she's laughing. Her laugh makes me want to laugh, too.

"Charl . . . ," she says.

Everyone in my family calls me Charl.

"I'm trying to be serious. Do you want to hear about this or not?"

I try to look serious, too, but it's no good.

Soon we're laughing so hard that Dad comes in to see what all the fuss is about. I guess my laugh is like a higher-pitched version of Mum's. Sometimes when we're laughing together, Dad puts his hands over his ears.

"I thought you two were meant to be doing some work," he says.

"We are," I tell him.

"Really?" he says, meaning "I don't believe a word of it."

He leaves us to it.

Mum takes a deep breath and wipes her eyes. "First of all," she says, "you were a beautiful baby. You had a very good appetite, and it's an absolute bloody miracle you're with us at all."

I was born a month after Mum's twentieth birthday.

"It was a very, very difficult birth. In the week before you were born, I'd had three false labors. At the time, I was living with your nan and bampy. It was Friday, February 21, 1986, when the labor pains started, and it must have been about one in the morning. By eight that morning they were coming every ten minutes. That's when I knew it was time.

"I went into Bampy and Nan's bedroom to tell them. Your nan told me to go back to sleep, but I knew you were coming.

" 'Mum. Really. I need to get to the hospital,' I said.

"It was a very cold February, and there was black ice on the roads, but Bampy drove me at top speed to St. David's Hospital. When we got to the hospital, I was made to sit in the waiting room with all the other expectant mums.

"The pain got worse.

"Then I was put in a bed on the labor ward, and I was in labor for most of the day. My friend Katherine came to visit, my mum was there, and so was Auntie Francis [Nan's sister], who got me hysterical with laughter, although I can't remember why.

"Anyway, by ten o'clock that night I still wasn't dilating, and the midwife didn't know why. I remember being in a lot of distress. Then, when it seemed it couldn't get any worse, I had an asthma attack. It was the first asthma attack I'd had since I was fourteen.

"I couldn't breathe. I remember feeling very panicked and frightened. I was attached to a monitor, and I can still remember watching your heartbeat getting slower and slower and slower until it stopped.

"Then — oh, my God, it was panic stations.

" 'Right, emergency cesarean now,' said the doctor, and that was it.

"I was put on a trolley, and they ran with me down the hall to the operating theater. I remember seeing the lights spinning overhead and seeing the faces of the doctors and nurses running alongside and hearing the double doors crashing open and closing behind us. Then a mask came over my face and someone said, 'Count to ten.'

"I got to three. The next thing I remember was waking up in the hall on a stretcher. A nurse was pushing me, and I turned to see you beside me in a crib.

"I remember feeling cheated. I had been through twenty-two hours of labor, and I even remember saying, 'I don't want a cesarean.' But I had no choice. Anyway, you were lucky to be alive. If we'd been living a hundred years ago, you wouldn't have made it. But I don't want to think about that. You were so beautiful. . . ."

25

"All right, Mum. You've already said that."

"But you were. Your skin was perfect. You're weren't wrinkly because you hadn't had all the stress of coming through the birth canal. . . ."

"Ugh."

"You weighed six pounds and fourteen ounces. You had startling blue eyes and rosebud lips. You were such a good feeder that I breast-fed you for fourteen months.

"When I took you home, though, I was still recovering from the cesarean and couldn't change a diaper. It was three days before I could lean over and change your diaper, and I remember feeling such a sense of achievement when I did it. . . ."

"Have you finished?"

"Oh, and when you were three weeks old, we had you christened by Father Delaney at the local parish church, St. Mary's."

Phew.

So there you have it.

I'm born.

My adopted dad, James Church, has brought me up since I was three and has legally adopted me, which is why I have his name.

Next I want to tell you about my hometown of Cardiff.

2

My Hometown

What should I say about Cardiff?

First of all, it's home and I love it because it's where I was born. I've visited a lot of other cities now, and — to be fair — Cardiff can't really compete with Los Angeles or Toronto. Still, I'm always really glad to come home when I've been away, though this has more to do with seeing my family and friends and sleeping in my own bed than the city itself.

Here are a few facts.

The Queen declared Cardiff the capital of Wales not that long ago, in 1955. And in May 1999 Cardiff was given a Welsh National Assembly, and now Wales has its own government. The new assembly building is in Cardiff Bay, which used to be called the docks of Tiger Bay.

I sang at the official opening of the Welsh

National Assembly with Tom Jones, who is also Welsh — I'm sure you knew that — and Shirley Bassey. I was only thirteen at the time, so I wasn't particularly interested in the politics of it all, but I was thrilled to take part. I met the Queen, Prince Philip, and Prince Charles, which was great. But I'll tell you about that later.

Other interesting facts about Cardiff off the top of my head?

It's like a smaller version of London with less pollution, and the Welsh people are really friendly. They will always give you the time of day. The Welsh are proud and close-knit, and you can never beat the Welsh — you can only score more points.

There are a lot of famous Welsh people. There's Richard Burton, Anthony Hopkins, Catherine Zeta-Jones, Tom Jones, Cerys from Catatonia, Rhys Ifans, and my mum's favorite bands, the Manic Street Preachers and the Stereophonics.

Once upon a time, Cardiff was the biggest coal-exporting port in the world. People from all over the world live here. The local beer is called Brains Bitter — it's disgusting according to Dad, who drinks lager — and there are over three thousand acres of park in Cardiff. That's a lot of trees and grass.

There's also fabulous music here.

We have the Welsh College of Music and Drama, which is where my singing teacher Lulu went, and the Welsh National Opera.

What are Cardiff's landmarks? Let me think.

Well, there's huge Cardiff Castle, sitting right in the middle of town and built on the site of an old Roman fort. The first inhabitants of Cardiff were Romans. Maybe that's why Roman history is my favorite part of history.

Since the Roman times, different bits of the castle have been added on every century. The castle has a little bit of everything. It has a moat and turrets and towers, and inside it's filled with antiques. And there are huge open-air concerts in the castle's grounds. We went to a concert there on Millennium Night.

Then there's Llandaff Cathedral.

The cathedral was originally built in the sixth century. It looks kind of spooky. Next door to it is the Cathedral School, where I went for two years.

Most of my childhood has been spent in Canton. It's the neighborhood next to Llandaff, and they're not that different, really. They have the same rows of houses with backyards and parks and local stores.

The Civic Centre is another landmark. It sits in Cathays Park and has fountains and trees all around it. It's very pretty. It's white with a dome and looks a little bit like Capitol Hill in Washington, D.C.

Cardiff also has a National Museum and Gallery, and in the archaeology section is a footprint left behind seven thousand years ago. Now that's ancient. I love history — especially ancient history — but I also love shopping.

Don't all teenage girls?

One of my favorite parts of Cardiff is the downtown area. Queen Street is very long and pedestrianized, and on Saturdays it's filled with teenagers and shoppers and musicians who play for money. There are circus performers and fair rides, carousels and dodgem cars, for the children.

Everywhere you go, you see signs for Cardiff's landmarks in English and Welsh.

Cathedral — *Eglwys Gadeiriol*

National Museum — *Amgueddfa G. Cymru*

Queen Street — *Heol y Frenhines*

In Cardiff the people speak English, not Welsh, and we learn Welsh not in school but in other parts of Wales — for instance, in Swansea, which is only forty miles away, they speak Welsh. But I sing in Welsh. It's a truly beautiful language.

From Queen Street you can see the ramparts of Cardiff Castle with all the flags flying. The Welsh flag is red with a blue cross. You can hear the sound of a local choir singing inside Cardiff Market.

On Saturdays the stores are packed with teenagers. There's a Virgin Megastore, which is great for CDs. There are loads of clothes and shoe stores and drugstores and cafés to hang out in. I go with my friends, and we spend the whole day together, wandering around and trying on stuff and drinking coffee.

Oh yes, how could I forget Cardiff's massive landmark — the Millennium Stadium? It was opened in 1999 for the Rugby World Cup, and I can't imagine Cardiff without it now. London has the Millennium Dome, but our stadium seats seventy-two thousand people, and wherever you are in Cardiff you can see it. It has red and white girders like stripes across the sky. Imagine a futuristic space station, the kind you see circling the earth in *Star Trek*, and you'll get the idea. It has a massive roof that slides back in the summer and stays closed in the winter.

The only other thing I need to say, just so you've got the full picture, is that Wales is very green and beautiful with hills and sea, and in the spring there are daffodils everywhere.

Cardiff also has lots of rain because it sits

underneath what's called a rain shadow. The city has mountains behind it, and the low clouds have to drop their rain before they can pass over the mountains. Cardiff gets the rain, and the other side doesn't.

But that's life, eh?

3

Meet My Mum

Now that you've got an idea of where I live, I want to introduce you to my mum and dad. After all, I wouldn't have a story to tell if it wasn't for Mum and Dad.

Mum first.

We're very close. We're both very argumentative, and she's very stubborn. I'm a Pisces, which is a water sign, and she's Aquarius, which is air, so I suppose what we do is earth each other. Somehow.

Mum's very small. She's five feet two and a half inches, and I've already caught up with her. I'm actually about to overtake her. Well, it wasn't difficult. Mum's very pretty and curvy, with wavy, chestnut-colored hair — although at the moment it's short and red and soft — that she straightens. She hates her curls and she hates the rain because when it rains her hair goes curly.

Her eyes are big and brown, and she makes them stand out with black mascara and brown eye pencil. Mum always tries to look her best. She never goes anywhere without her makeup.

Auntie Caroline and I love makeup, too, but we don't wear it all the time like Mum. I've picked up some cool beauty tips from Mum and from the makeup artists I've worked with. Natural is the best look for me. Golden shiny cheeks, pale eye shadows, and lip stains that make your lips glossy with just a tinge of red. Mum likes dark, matte lipsticks in plums and browns. When she was a teenager she wore black lipstick. I can't imagine wanting to go out with black lips.

Mum dresses very well.

She always looks classy and groomed. She doesn't go for wearing casual stuff, sneakers and baggy T-shirts and leggings. She wears nice trouser suits and high heels. Her hair is always done, and she doesn't like anyone to see her looking a mess.

Mum was born Maria Cooper on January 28, 1966.

Her dad, Gary (Yes, Gary Cooper, just like the film star), was a plasterer by trade but a rock 'n' roller by nature. I've already told you that I call him Bampy, but more of him later. Mum's mum, my nan, served lunches in the cafeteria at a local school.

Mum was born in a district near Cardiff's docks called Splott.

When my mum was four and Auntie Caroline was two, the family moved from Splott to Canton. Canton is only a few miles away from Splott, but it's a prettier part of Cardiff. It's a lovely, residential neighborhood with lots of trees and families, and it's five to ten minutes from Cardiff's city center. Canton has a main street where everyone does their shopping and stops for a gossip. It's a friendly place, and it feels safe.

In the middle of Canton is Victoria Park. It has flowerbeds full of roses and petunias in the summer and a playground with swings and a slide. Bampy used to take me there when I was little. Whenever I'm at home and I've got time, I take my nephew Elliot, who's five.

Nan and Bampy still live in the same house that Maria and Auntie Caroline were brought up in. Auntie Caroline lives five minutes away, and if she's not at home, she's at Nan's house — usually curled up on the settee with a mug of tea.

The interesting thing about Bampy is that before he had a family, he had a band. Even when Mum was growing up, there were always musical instruments lying around the house. Bampy had electric guitars and a saxophone, and Mum says that Bampy was always playing a tune — sometimes until one or two in the morning with his friend Mickey G. Mickey G was an electric guitarist who played with Eric Clapton and Tom Jones.

Mum was brought up with music.

She says that she and Auntie Caroline were never pushed musically but that their interests came naturally. When Mum was eight she picked up a guitar, Bampy taught her a few chords, and she joined a local folk group in the church. When Mum was thirteen she asked to have guitar lessons.

Mum had the musical ability, but it was Auntie Caroline who had the voice. When Caroline was sixteen, she got up in a local pub on one of their singalong nights and sang Elton John's "I'm Still Standing."

She's been a singer ever since.

By the time Mum was eighteen, she had passed all her eight grades in music.

Then she quit.

She shakes her head when she talks about it.

Bampy was devastated.

"I hurt my dad [Bampy] really badly when I gave it up," she says. "I broke his heart. He said 'Why?' and I said, 'I just haven't got it in me anymore.' You've got to be very dedicated to play an instrument."

But you see, Mum was interested in other things like pop bands and her friends. She says that when she was at school (the old Bishop Hannon in Pentrebance, which was pulled down many years ago), she already wore makeup and her hair in ponytails, one above each ear.

"They used to moan at me about it [makeup], but in the end they let me wear it," she says.

Mum was a bit of a rebel. She says it runs in the family.

"The Coopers always were a confident lot," she says. "I think you've inherited some of this — but it's not obnoxious confident or over-the-top-get-on-your-nerves confident. It's just that we're comfortable with ourselves as people."

Mum liked to be different. She says she craved attention, which I suppose is another thing I've inherited from her. According to Mum, the style in the mid-eighties was "new romantic," which suited her down to the ground.

I've seen photographs. They were scary.

The way she looked was totally over the top — lots of big hair and wild makeup. Mum used to wear frilly skirts and hats with brims. She was really into eighties music like Spandau Ballet and Japan and David Bowie. Her musical tastes haven't influenced me at all. I'm not into any of that eighties stuff, even though it's all coming back.

"I didn't enjoy school very much," she says. "I didn't like studying, even though the teachers were wonderful."

In the end she finished with one A-Level in music.

In my family *everyone* loves music.

Let me introduce you to the rest of them.

First of all, there's Auntie Francis, who likes to sing "Crazy" and "Jerusalem" at family get-togethers. She's Nan's sister. She has four children: Linda, Paul, Susan, and Alison.

Linda had Nadine first.

She has a fabulous voice. We used to sing "Chick, chick, chick, chick, chicken, lay a little egg for me . . ." We were a great double act. Paul's daughter Jenna is a year younger than me. Paul and his wife, Ann-Marie, also have Shannon, Carly, and Steven. Susan has Abbie, and Alison has Michael.

Finally there's Elliot, who's also blessed with a singing voice. You should hear him singing along to Queen's "We Will Rock You." What a little star. And he's started at the Cathedral School, which is where I went.

People always ask if I come from a stage family, and the answer is no — but we've always loved singing. I mean, all my aunties like to sing.

Nan says it comes from her side of the family, too. She says that her dad — my great-granddad — was a big fan of Hollywood musicals. He used to take her and her sister to the movies every Saturday.

"That's when the cinema was *the* entertainment," she says.

They would go and watch Fred Astaire and Ginger Rogers and Bing Crosby and Gene Kelly singing in the rain. Nan's dad loved to sing himself, she says. He was always whistling a tune or singing a song.

Nan also talks about Auntie Ilene, who was her aunt. I never met her because she passed away before I was born, but she had an operatic voice. Her party piece was "One Fine Day" from *Madame Butterfly*.

Nan still talks about it. I would have loved to hear it.

Today, whenever the family get together for Christmas, birthdays, or a special occasion, someone will always sing a song. Everyone does a turn, and it's always been like that.

So I guess I'm confident on stage because

it's what I'm used to. I've been performing since I was three.

According to Mum, "You were bright from an early age. I can't say you had a particularly loud set of lungs, because that all started when you were three and first started to sing in earnest. But you *always* used to sing along to the radio, which was the first sign we had that you were gifted in that direction."

When Mum finished school she planned to go to college. Instead, at the last minute she decided she would rather go out into the big wide world. She got a job as a clerical assistant in the local tax office. It was hardly a load of laughs, but she stuck it out by promising herself it would only be a temporary thing.

And there were boys to think about. Mum loved going out.

"Most of my boyfriends didn't last more than a couple of months," she says. "My group of friends were actually good Catholic girls."

Then she met Dad.

You know, the funny thing about Mum and Dad's story is that they were actually brought up two streets apart in Canton.

Dad says he remembers knocking on Mum's door when he was about sixteen years old to ask if they needed their windows cleaned. He was trying to earn a bit of extra pocket money. He says that when Mum answered his knock, she poked her head round the door, looked at him suspiciously, and wouldn't speak to him.

Mum doesn't remember him at all.

When they met properly, years later, Mum was twenty-three and Dad was twenty-five.

If you really want to hear the whole story, though, maybe you should hear it from them. I think it's a bit embarrassing, actually, very embarrassing. They don't think so. Mum is smiling. She likes telling this story. It's a story I've heard a million times before.

"You know where I met your dad, don't you?"

"Just get on with it, Mum."

"Okay, there's no need to be cheeky. It was in a bar called Quinnies, where everyone went for a late night drink. There was a keyboard player, and people would turn up with backing tapes or guitars, and people would get up and give a song.

"I very nearly hadn't gone out that night. My best friend, Geraldine, said she was too tired, so I phoned my friend Mary and said, 'Come on, Mary.'

" 'Do I have to?' she said.

" 'Please.'

"In the end she agreed.

"We got to Quinnies really late, and I got talking to James's friend, whom I knew from work. Then I said, 'Well, aren't you going to introduce me to your friend?' and he introduced me to James. James was a bit tipsy, but I remember him asking what I was doing later that week and I said nothing special, so I wrote down my number and put it in the top pocket of his shirt. He was wearing a light denim shirt.

"I wanted to see him again, but I remember thinking, I wonder if I'll ever see him again? Well, a couple of days later he phoned. He had found my telephone number but couldn't for the life of him remember my name. He rang the office and asked for Mary. Luckily Mary figured it out and said, 'Oh, you want Maria.'

"When I got on the phone he asked me out and we arranged to meet that evening at a local pub. We actually arranged to meet *outside* the pub. You see, he couldn't remember what I looked like.

"All he could remember about me was my bright red lipstick.

"We met.

"And, well, a first date is a first date, and I was a bit nervous. We chatted. It was a bit awkward, but I found him very attractive, charming, funny. Tall, dark, and handsome, basically. . . ."

Dad has appeared with two cups of tea. "Am I interrupting something?"

"Get out!"

That was Mum and me shouting together.

"Dad, you can tell your story later on."

Dad laughs and gives us our tea.

"Thanks, Dad."

He's gone.

Here's Mum again.

"Me and your dad started meeting once or twice a week, and it went from there, really. I'd been seeing him about a month when I introduced him to you. You were three. It was fine. He was great about you, nice and easy. Really lovely. Anyway, that first twelve months with James, we had our ups and downs, but it was at this point we said, What are we going to do? Are we going to try living together?

"What brought it to a head was that before he met me he had applied for a visa to go and work in Australia for a year. Then, suddenly, the visa came through. He really wanted to go, and I said, 'Fine, but don't expect me to be waiting for you when you come back.'

"So he didn't go.

"At that time he was living in a rented flat,

43

and I was still back living with your nan and bampy. Fortunately your dad had some shares from a previous job. So he cashed those in and we used the money to buy a little house together on Glamorgan Street in Canton, five minutes from your nan's house and five minutes from Auntie Francis's house.

"From then on I was back in full-time work."

Okay, I can carry on from here.

What happened next was that Mum got a job as a housing officer. She was working for the Cardiff local government. Her job was to visit families who lived on the estates on the outskirts of town. It was a tough job, and she had to deal with a lot of nasty people.

What I remember is her coming home from work exhausted. She would get on the telephone and call up all her girlfriends and moan about her job and moan about the people she had to go and deal with.

She moaned a lot. She hated her job.

Mum is nodding her head. She doesn't look happy.

"It was the type of job you brought home with you. I had to go and visit families who had fallen behind with rent payments or were causing a nuisance and upsetting the neighbors. I even had to go to people's houses and tell them to get out if they couldn't afford to live there anymore. Sometimes it was heart-breaking. I'd see four-year-olds walking the streets on their own. I would knock on doors and have kids as young as six answer. When I asked, 'Where's your mum?' they just said, 'She's out, miss.'

"I saw girls your age pregnant, smoking, and drinking. I know it influenced the way I brought you up. Of course, my own mum, your nan, is very strict and moral. She's also a wonderful, loving mum. I learned so much from her when I had you."

By this time I had started primary school (elementary school) in Canton. The school is called St. Mary's. I had to be at school at eight fifty-five in the morning, but Mum had to be at work at eight-thirty, and so did Auntie Linda.

Mum and Auntie Linda used to drop off me and my cousin Nadine at Auntie Francis's house. Auntie Francis lived two doors down from the school, you see. Then just before the bell went at eight fifty-five, Auntie Francis would put on our coats and walk us to school.

Mum's job kept her out until at least five o'clock every afternoon, but school finished at three-thirty. So after school Nan or Auntie Caroline, who was still living with

Nan and Bampy, would come and pick us up and we would go and have tea at Nan's house.

Somehow Mum lasted eight years in that job.

She had to deal with a lot of abusive language and angry people, but it wasn't all bad. She made a lot of good friends while she was there. She still loves going off to meet all the girls in work.

Mum smiles. "As a matter of fact, I'm going to see the girls next week," she says. "It's always good to catch up on office gossip."

Mum quit her job as a housing officer in December 1998 when my first album came out. Now she travels with me. Dad remained in his job for another year before circumstances changed, and now Dad travels with us, too.

They're learning quickly about the music business. Dad's more of an organizer than Mum. He gets my music and my clothes and my passport together. He drives us everywhere because Mum's terrified of motorways. Dad also cooks because Mum burns everything, even fish fingers.

But Mum's brilliant at the business side. She works out my school schedule and my schedule with Sony and my management team.

Mum thinks we're especially close because I'm an only child. She says she still might have another child. I'd like it if she did. I'd like to have a brother or a sister when I'm older, although I don't really think of myself as an only child because I've got Elliot.

Still, Mum thinks that because we spend so much time together traveling, we've become even closer. She's probably right. It's true that we do everything together — not that it means I tell her everything that's going through my head, because I don't.

It's also good to have Dad as a chaperon, because even though Dad is strict, he keeps things fun. He's the one who makes me scream and laugh, which drives Mum crazy because she thinks it'll damage my voice. But she knows that I have to release a bit of tension sometimes when most of the time I'm completely in control and on show.

And, to be honest, I do get fed up sometimes traveling with my parents, but it's getting easier. Mum is more relaxed with me now I'm getting older. She says she's not worried for me anymore. She says she's confident that I'll choose whatever's best for me. She's quite happy to sit back and not get worked up about everything I do anymore.

Singing and touring the world is hard work, but so is being a teenager. I still fight with Mum. She gets at me about tidying my room.

"It looks like World War Three in here," she says.

She gets at me about what I eat.

"No more chocolate."

She nags me about doing my homework and decides what time I have to be home from my friends' houses.

Working together can interfere with being mother and daughter, but I always know when Mum's in a bad mood, and she's the same with me. In the end, we *always* work it out.

I wouldn't have it any other way.

4

Mad for Dad

All girls love their dads, right?

I know I do. My dad's very tall. He's six feet two and a half. He has dark brown hair and the same color eyes as mine, sort of greenish blue. I suppose you could say he's athletic. He used to play a lot of rugby until he injured his back and had to give it up.

He looks pretty fit, considering. I suppose he's good-looking. It's hard to say when he's your dad, but I know all my friends think he is. He even did some modeling in his twenties, and he looks younger than thirty-six.

Come to think of it, he'd make a great singer in a boy band, although, I almost forgot, Dad *can't* sing.

The thing about Dad is he's always got a joke. He can make light of anything, even when I'm stressed out. He will make a face or say something weird, it only has to be one word, and I'll crack up laughing — which always makes me feel better.

Dad's come in wearing beige combat pants and a black T-shirt and — surprise, surprise — he's bringing me a nice cup of tea.

"Dad, what are your hobbies?"

"Rugby . . ."

"Yes. I've told them that."

"Going to the pub."

"You're good at having a good time, you mean."

"Bird-watching, and I mean the ones with the feathers . . ."

"Please . . ."

That's one of his jokes, by the way.

"Watching films, especially war films."

"Okay, you can go now. That's enough."

He's gone.

I suppose if I had to describe my dad, I'd say he's very loving and very kind. He's very gentle, but he can be grumpy, although not for very long, and he loses his temper like everyone else. He likes to go out with the boys and get away from me and Mum, but who can blame him?

Dad's got a great attitude to life. He's had all sorts of different jobs, and they have given him a good perspective on things, which I like to remember. Dad explains it, kind of seriously, like this.

"The jobs showed me the variety of life. I've seen good and bad. I think it helps me appreciate what you're doing, and it means I can tell you about how difficult it is for most people who have had to start at the bottom and work their way up."

I think it makes sense.

Dad was born on August 21, 1964, at St. David's Hospital. Yes, the same hospital I was born in. Dad's dad, Dave, was a truck driver, and his mother, Jean, comes from Yorkshire, which is in the north of England. Dad has a brother, David, who is four years older than him, but I don't see this side of the family as much as Mum's side.

In 1970, when Dad was six years old, his dad announced one day over breakfast that they were immigrating to Australia. Back then for ten pounds you could take the whole family to Australia. The next thing Dad remembers was being on an airplane with a couple of suitcases and absolutely no idea where they were going.

They arrived in a town called Brisbane.

They stayed in a big camp for new arrivals, and they were there for six months. The camp was filled with rows and rows of wooden huts that according to Dad weren't much bigger than our living room at our house in Llandaff, which was about twelve feet by twelve. There was no kitchen in the hut, and they had to go to a big canteen for meals.

Dad's father got a job as a prison officer in a prison on the outskirts of Brisbane, and the family moved to a bungalow. Dad shared a bedroom with his brother. He says it was a happy time.

"I had a very happy childhood, but Australia was a young boy's dream come true," says Dad. "From our bedroom we looked out at a valley that stretched as far as the eye could see. There was so much wildlife. Every Australian animal you imagine lived out there. We were woken up by the sounds of all the animals. It was like living in a jungle."

Often in the mornings Dad would look out the window and find a kangaroo in the garden just a few feet away. He and his brother went barefoot most of the time, and they wore shorts to school.

He says the other boys taught them how to catch lizards and snakes and spiders. Most of them were poisonous, but boys don't really care about things like that. Not that I'm afraid of lizards or snakes or spiders. When I was younger I wanted a tarantula, but Mum wouldn't let me. She was worried she would step on it. Instead I got a lizard — a water dragon, actually — called

Iggy. I had to feed him live insects, which I somehow got used to; but when I started traveling it wasn't fair to keep him, so I gave him to Jeff, my driver, to look after. Whenever I'm back in Cardiff I go and visit Iggy at Jeff's house.

I know I'm way too old to have a crush on a lizard, but Iggy's kind of cute. You'd think so, too, if you met him.

Anyway, at night Dad and his brother used to creep out under the stars and play soldiers in the dark. The only problem was that there were these giant, six-inch king toads that hopped about in the grass, croaking like mad. You couldn't see them.

"If you've ever trodden on a toad with your bare feet and squashed it flat, you'll never forget it," says Dad. Then he makes a loud popping sound with his finger in his mouth. It's disgusting.

"Ugh!" I scream.

Dad thinks it's hilarious to make me scream.

Early last year, spring 2000, we went to Australia as part of a big promotional tour I did. We visited Sydney, which was breathtakingly beautiful, but we didn't get to Brisbane. Even so, it was enough to be back on Australian ground for Dad to go off on all his stories. Again.

"Did I ever tell you about the giant king toads —"

"*Yes!*"

Dad's family stayed out in Australia for two years, and they moved three times. But when Dad's grandmother died — that's his mum's mum — his mum decided she wanted to come home for the funeral. They packed up and returned to Cardiff and, like I said, the family ended up living two streets away from Mum in Canton.

"As soon as we arrived back we realized we'd made a big mistake. We'd had a very good lifestyle out in Australia, but it was too late," says Dad.

They were back in Cardiff for good.

Dad and his brother started at a local school. Not that Dad spent much time at school. According to him, he was a bit of a "Jack the lad." In other words, he was a bit of a wild card.

Dad decided early on that he didn't really want to go to school. He came up with a scheme for "mitching" — or playing truant. He would arrive at school every morning in time for assembly at nine o'clock. He would answer his name at roll call and then slip out when the lessons began.

When everyone else was learning math, English, and French, Dad would be off at the local park, playing football with a bunch of boys.

Other times he says, "We'd wait until our parents went out to work, then drop into each other's houses."

The only times Dad went to school was for the rugby and football matches — or for gym classes. It's hard to believe, but Dad was actually very good at gymnastics.

He didn't pass any of his exams.

It was hardly surprising.

Dad left school age fifteen and a half and went straight into a job in a factory. He was there for eight years.

"It was hell," he says. "It was a horrible place to work."

I think this is why my schooling is so important to Dad. He doesn't want me to waste my school years or miss out like he did.

The factory he worked in made cakes for all the big supermarkets in England and Wales. Dad did every sort of job there, from working in the warehouse, packing and driving, to working in the ovens. When he was working in the ovens, he had to start at seven-thirty in the morning and he was there until two or three the next morning. They were very long shifts, and it was very hard work.

When Dad was twenty-four years old, he quit this job.

He went from the factory to driving trucks around west and middle Wales for three years. He was made redundant from this job not long after moving into the Glamorgan Street house with me and Mum.

This was when Dad had his first taste of the music world. Dad didn't have a musical family like ours. He says that when he was my age he was into punk and the Clash and the Stranglers.

Not my kind of music at all.

Dad's real introduction to music, then, was through meeting the Cooper family. Next thing he knew, he was off to work for Auntie Caroline, driving her to pubs and clubs all around the Welsh valleys as a "roadie."

Dad explains, "It was my job to do the driving and set up the sound system. What Caroline was doing would be extremely hard for any singer to do. She was trying to sing while the people in the pubs were out to enjoy themselves. She had to deal with drunk people shouting and joking. They were noisy and rowdy, and she was trying to sing over them.

"The worst occasion was a gig in a village in the middle of nowhere where Caroline was singing for a wedding party. Someone said something they shouldn't have, and World War Three broke out. It was a huge brawl with tables and chairs flying. It was like something from the Wild West. The police were called, and I had to get Caroline out of there in a hurry."

I think it was bit of an eye-opener for Dad. And he decided something *very* important.

"I knew that this was the last thing in the world I wanted for you," he says. "No offense to Caroline, who is better than those places anyway, but no daughter of mine was going to end up singing in pubs and clubs."

I started singing when I was three. I started singing in talent competitions in clubs and halls when I was eight. But as soon as I was old enough, Mum sent me to singing lessons and, well, you'll just have to keep reading the book to find out the rest.

To finish Dad's story, he went from working with Auntie Caroline to working in a factory that made machine parts. He hated that job.

His next job, though, he really liked.

He joined a security installation firm. It was the Cardiff branch of Specialist Property Services, and the company made steel shutters to protect houses on big estates — or projects — when they were repossessed and to protect shops from vandals.

Within a month Dad was promoted to the position of foreman for the southwest. He had twenty men working for him, and they were on call twenty-four hours a day to answer emergencies. Dad had to travel all over Wales, and like Mum, he had to deal with some pretty rough areas and desperate people.

He says he felt sorry for some of the people, but he was there to do a job. He was good at his job, and he enjoyed the responsibility. But he missed seeing me and Mum, because what had happened during the last year of his job was that my first album, *Voice of an Angel*, had been released. And suddenly I was traveling all over the world with Mum while Dad was working all over Wales.

Dad says, "I felt I was missing out on seeing you grow up. I didn't see you or Maria for almost twelve months, and you were growing up so quickly. I was away for weeks on end. I would be lonely and would look forward to seeing you when you got back from traveling. Then you would arrive back after three weeks burned out and all you wanted to do was relax and sit in the house, and I wanted to take you out.

"I finally had a successful job with long hours and good pay, but I felt I was losing touch with my wife and daughter. Then when I spoke to both of you about my feelings, you said you felt the same way.

"The final crunch was when your manager at the time lost his personal assistant and was looking for another one, wasn't it? That's when we said, Instead of paying out another salary to someone new, why don't I come on board. And now you get to have me around all the time which you love, don't you?"

"Not."

Just joking.

Like I said, Dad and I have the same wicked sense of humor. I can't imagine traveling without him.

"Yes, we're both a bit wicked," says Dad. "When you're doing your warm-up exercises, I join in. . . ."

"Yes — you *think* you're being really helpful, Dad."

"You're trying to teach me, but I think I'm a lost cause."

"I *know* you're a lost cause."

Mum and I would be lost without Dad.

We would never get to the airport on time if it wasn't for Dad — and I would never remember where I left my mobile phone. One time I couldn't find it, and Dad found it in the shower. I was still talking to my friend Kim when I got in.

"And then you couldn't work out why it didn't work. You said it was the battery, so I opened it and all this water poured out."

"Yes. All right. I was talking —"

"You're dizzy like that."

Which is why I've got Dad. Thank God for Dad.

5

When James Met Maria

Now that you've met my dad, I suppose the next thing to do is let him tell his story about how he met Mum. There are two sides to every story, and since I've allowed Mum to tell hers, I'd better let Dad do the same.

"I suppose the first thing to say is that I met your mum on a Sunday night, and I *never, ever, ever* go out on Sunday nights. But I was with a friend who wanted to go, and on this one occasion, for some reason, I agreed.

"Back then pubs closed at ten-thirty on Sunday nights, but he mentioned this club called Quinnies, where they had a late license.

"When we got to Quinnies, to be perfectly honest, I'd had a few too many beers. Anyway, we see these two girls and get chatting to them because my friend happens to know Maria. I actually took a shine to Maria's friend Mary, but she didn't want to know, so I turned my attention to Maria.

"I asked Maria for her telephone number, and I said I'd call her. The next day I found this number in my pocket. All I could remember about Maria was that she had bright red lipstick on. I called her office, but I got the wrong name. I asked for Mary, not Maria, so Mary came on the phone.

"I said, 'This is James. Remember me from Sunday? You said to give you a call.'

"Mary laughed and said, 'No, I didn't. You want Maria, not me.'

"Then Maria got on the telephone. We arranged to go for a drink at a pub that evening, but I said we should meet in the carpark because otherwise I wouldn't recognize her."

"No, you never."

That was Mum.

"And your mum had on this baggy outfit . . ."

"That's true. I was staying at my friend Geraldine's house that night, and I had to borrow a pair of her jeans that were too big. And you told me later that at first you didn't know if you wanted to see me again."

"That's true."

"And it was only when we went back to Geraldine's house later on that night and you saw me have a giggle with my friends and loosen up that you thought I was okay."

Dad is nodding.

"You made me laugh, and that's what it's all about, right? I mean, you made me laugh inside. I suppose I felt very comfortable around you right from the start. We became close very quickly, and you became my best friend. I could be myself with you."

He also liked the way Mum spoke her mind.

"What I liked about you, other than that you dressed to kill . . ."

I think Mum's blushing.

". . . was that you enjoyed life. You said exactly what you felt, and there were no airs and graces. Here was this very petite, smart young girl with bright red lipstick and a voluptuous figure, always a lady — and then you would suddenly come out with these unbelievable things. You were like one of the boys."

And we all know how much Dad likes going out with the boys.

Now this is what Dad has to say about meeting me for the first time.

"The next weekend, I went to meet you and your mum in town for lunch. You were three going on four, and you were very bubbly and pretty, chatting away and wanting to know everyone's business. You were a delightful child and a pleasure to be around."

"Yes. Okay . . ."

"Then, as my relationship with Maria grew, so it did with you. It's difficult to remember my life without you two. From the beginning I was welcomed into the Cooper family, and now Maria's parents are like second parents to me."

When I was six Mum and Dad decided to get married.

They were both secure in their jobs and, well, Mum wanted a ring on her finger.

They were married in the local church in Canton on Romily Road. It's a huge church with steps leading up to it and stained-glass windows and big trees on both sides. Sixty guests were invited, and to keep it traditional, the night before the wedding Mum and I spent the night at Nan and Bampy's house, while Dad stayed by himself in our house.

Although I'm skipping ahead here.

A few weeks before the wedding, Mum had a hen night at the local Churchill Hotel with all her best girlfriends. Auntie Caroline was singing there that night.

The next week, Dad had a stag night with his mates at the rugby club and — despite Mum's misgivings — he made it home safe and sound. The wedding was only days away.

6
Wedding Bells

Saturday, May 9, 1992.

You only have to look at the photographs on the living room wall to see what a happy wedding day Mum and Dad had. Everyone is smiling, although the weather was awful. There was fog in the morning and gale-force winds all afternoon.

Not that anyone noticed.

The wedding was due to take place at one o'clock in the afternoon. Back at home, Dad told us later that he'd calmed his nerves with a stiff drink. He also had his best man, Manuel Batolo, there.

Then Dad's brother arrived, he was an usher, and they all went off to the church. They were an hour early. The church was empty except for one member of the clergy.

"Well, there's only one thing for it," said Dad, and they headed straight across the road to the pub.

As the hour passed, without realizing it, Dad and the boys were soon joined by almost the entire wedding party. The bar was packed. Everybody was in high spirits and having a laugh when Auntie Caroline appeared at the door in her bridesmaid dress, looking, says Mum, "like the Sugar Plum Fairy." She was wearing a pink dress with a hooped skirt.

She was furious.

"What are you doing here?" she shouted at everyone. "Maria's sitting in the car outside the church, and there's no one in there. Get in there *now*. All of you!"

I was also a bridesmaid, and so was cousin Nadine.

I wore a little white dress and curls in my hair, and I carried a bouquet of pink and purple silk roses. I was sitting in the Rolls-Royce with Mum and Bampy, and I can remember seeing everyone pile out of the pub and run across the road. Dad led the way, looking sheepish, and everyone waved as they passed.

"Hi, Maria. Hello, Charlotte."

Mum sat beneath her veil, cursing Dad's name. Then she calmed down.

Minutes later, with everyone in their seats and the organist playing the "Wedding

March," Mum was led down the aisle by Bampy, with us bridesmaids behind.

Mum looked fabulous. Her dress was shell pink, sequined, with a full skirt puffed up with lots of tulle petticoats. She was wearing a tiara and a full-length veil and carrying the biggest bouquet you've ever seen.

I think she looked like a princess.

She thinks she looked like Scarlett O'Hara.

When we reached the end of the aisle where the minister was standing, the minister turned and said to Bampy, "Who gives this woman —"

He didn't even get to finish his sentence before Bampy, thinking it was showtime and he was on stage, threw open his arms, took a deep bow, and said in a very loud voice:

"I do!"

The whole congregation burst out laughing.

And that was just the start of it.

Dad then began having real problems.

First of all, he kept having to ask the minister to repeat everything — slowly, please — because he couldn't catch it. Then, funnier still, when the minister came to ask him to say the line about "lawful impediment," he caught Dad out completely.

Dad tried at least ten times to get it out — "Impedi . . . Impedi . . . Impedi" — but in the end he gave up and the minister had to say it for him.

As you can imagine, no one could stop laughing, including me. I had a fit of giggles and almost dropped my posy.

Then we went to the reception.

The reception was at the Fairwater Labour Club, which was nearby. There was lots of food and drink and a DJ with a mobile disco. He was French and didn't speak English very well. He also preferred slow songs to fast ones.

Mum had enough of smoochy dancing and wanted to get the disco going. She went up to the DJ and said, "Can you *up* the tempo?"

He nodded and turned a knob. The music got louder, but the beat stayed the same. Mum went back.

"Up tempo! Up tempo!" she said.

More nods. More volume. Mum repeated herself, and the same thing happened again. The music got louder and louder until it was so loud that people couldn't hear themselves speak.

Mum gave up.

That's when we decided to make our own music.

Auntie Caroline went first. She sang "I Am What I Am" by Shirley Bassey. She sang so beautifully that everyone had tears in their eyes.

Cousin Paul went next and did his Elvis impersonation with plenty of wobbly knees and wobbly voice. One of Mum's friends sang "I knew the Bride When She Used to Rock 'n' Roll," and Bampy did one of his old rock 'n' roll tunes.

What did I sing?

Nadine and I did our favorite "Chick, Chick, Chick, Chick, Chicken" song, of course.

As Mum likes to say, "It was a magical night."

As for Mum and Dad's honeymoon, the less said the better, really. They chose a package holiday to Crete, and everything that could go wrong did go wrong. The plane was delayed. The luggage got lost. The hotel was tacky, and the pool looked like a muddy pond. They couldn't see the bottom of it.

Then — yes, you've guessed it — it rained.

But Mum and Dad can have fun wherever they are.

Even so, they were happy to get home, and I was happy to see them.

And now that we've been to so many amazing countries, they probably feel quite mushy about those rainy days in Crete.

7

School Days

When I was four I started school at St. Mary's Catholic Primary School in Canton where we used to live. It's a gray brick building with tarmac playgrounds and baskets of red geraniums hanging in front. It's the same school Mum and Auntie Caroline went to.

We even shared a few of the same teachers.

One of the teachers was Sister Leonie, who is a nun and wears a habit and has a very strong Irish accent. She used to scold us for talking, but we liked her even though she was strict.

What can I remember about my first day at St. Mary's? Not very much, to be honest.

Well, I was only four.

When Mum went to St. Mary's, she didn't have to wear a uniform. When I went, I had to wear a blue sweatshirt with "St. Mary's" on the front. I remember walking past the big blue railings and through the big blue gates to become one of the 250 children between the ages of four and eleven who went to St. Mary's.

I loved school right from the start.

My best friend's name was Samantha O'Grady, and I remember idolizing her. I thought she was the most beautiful little girl that I had ever met. She had black eyes and long black hair, and sometimes after school we would go to her house and play in the garden.

We would always play catch — you know, the game where you have to catch the other person. But our favorite game of all was kiss catch, which we played with the boys at school. The playgrounds used to be divided with one for the boys and one for the girls, but by the time we were there the playground was communal. Kiss catch was more about catching the boys and punching them, not kissing them, but then it all meant the same thing.

Our other favorite game was squashing each other on the bench. We could fit four of us on the bench, two in the middle and one on either side. The two at the side of the bench had to move in as far as they could and squash the others. I know it sounds silly, but then it was lots of fun.

I changed schools when I was ten and I lost touch with Samantha, but I still have lots of happy memories.

Our headmaster's name was Mr. Jefferies.

Mr. Jefferies is still the headmaster of St. Mary's. He has gray hair, a mustache, and watery blue eyes. He can be funny when he wants to be and severe at other times. His office is painted creamy white and has lots of bookshelves filled with religious books like the *Book of Saints*. There is something special about his office.

It's a quiet place.

We had to be at school every morning by eight fifty-five. Like I said, Auntie Francis used to drop cousin Nadine and me off at school because Mum had to be at work before school started.

In the mornings before class began, we would always say a prayer. Once a week, on Fridays, we had assembly in the hall. Mr. Jefferies would tell a funny story and read something from the Bible to educate us on gospel values. One Easter I remember Mr. Jefferies put on a tape and pretended to do a striptease. He unbuttoned his shirt, and underneath on his vest were lots of Easter ducks. It was hysterical.

Music was very important at St. Mary's.

In assembly we sang hymns like "All

Things Bright and Beautiful."

I was in the school choir, and I had the same choir teacher as Mum. Her name was Mrs. Guinea. She was about ninety years old (well, she seemed that old to us), and she used to wear her hair in long braids wrapped around her head. She would thump out songs for us to sing to on the piano in the hall.

Once we went to sing songs at an old people's home. The old people were sitting in armchairs, and some of them were fast asleep.

My favorite teacher was Miss Hogan, who taught me for a year when I was six. She had a kind face and a soft voice. She taught us songs I've never forgotten. We used to sing the Carol King song "You've Got a Friend," ("You just call out my name, And you know wherever I am, I'll come running to see you again . . .")

Do you know the one?

Then one day my friend Jeanine and I somehow found out that Miss Hogan's name was Adele. We were in the playground and we found a ladybird and we decided to call it Adele. We were very proud of our ladybird and wanted to tell Miss Hogan what we had done. We went and found her and showed it to her. We told her that its name was Adele.

73

She gave us a very strange look and said, "That's a silly name. Why did you call it that?"

I thought it was a strange thing for her to say.

When I was eight I decided I wanted to learn to play the violin. I only played it for a year. I was terrible at it and Mum hated the noise of me practicing and I hated practicing. I had to play "Twinkle, Twinkle, Little Star" at a school concert, and I completely messed it up. That was when I decided I'd had enough. I was never going to make it as a violinist.

Besides, by the time I was eight I had started singing and dancing lessons after school hours. I had started dancing lessons every Tuesday with a lady called Lisa Meggitt who taught ballet, tap, and modern jazz.

And I was performing in musicals.

I nearly got the part of Annie.

It was Mum who spotted the auditions for a production of *Annie* being put on by a local drama group at St. Peter's Hall. It was advertised in the local newspaper.

I was very late to audition. The drama group had already auditioned hundreds of other girls, but as Mum says, "Then along came this little girl with this huge voice," meaning me. I ended up getting the part of Molly, who is one of the other orphans, and I loved every minute of it.

Then there were the church socials.

One of the ways St. Mary's Church helps raise funds for repairs and upkeep is to put on church socials twice a year. These are evenings of singing, dancing, comedy, and magic performed by groups of local kids for their parents and the public.

Auntie Caroline used to help organize the church socials, and it was Dad's job to videotape them. I want to die when I watch the videos now, but I can't tell you how much I loved doing those church shows at the time.

I've made myself watch one of the videos so that I can describe it to you. It's so embarrassing to watch. I'm nine, and I think I am fabulous. I think I'm a disco diva. I'm wearing black thigh-length socks and a miniskirt and big silver earrings borrowed from a friend of my mum's, and my hair is up in a bunch on the top of my head.

In Wales it's called a-little-bit-up-a-little-bit-down style.

I'm singing "Gloria," and I'm belting it out.

You see, before I started singing lessons with my teacher Lulu — whom you're about to meet — which wasn't long after doing this church show, I used to sing like Auntie Caroline.

What I mean is, I had a belting voice or a chest voice like Celine Dion or Whitney Houston. I've always been able to hit the high notes.

Back to the video.

I'm doing a hip swivel. I've got one arm wrapped round my waist and the other up high above my head.

Auntie Caroline taught me all her stage moves.

And now we're all disco dancing on the stage, and I'm moving so fast, you wouldn't believe it. I used to be quite small for my age.

It was only five years ago. It's incredible how much has happened since.

When I was nine Mr. Jefferies asked me to sing in assembly.

I sang a song called "Suo Gân," a Welsh song that ended up on the first album.

I recently went back to St. Mary's to say hello to Mr. Jefferies, and I was really touched to see that the signed poster of *Voice of an Angel* that I'd given the school had been pinned up in the entrance foyer. Sitting in Mr. Jefferies office — which hasn't changed a bit — listening to all the children laughing and screaming outside in the playground, I asked him what he remembered of that assembly when I sang "Suo Gân."

"I can tell you that at the end of your song, you could have heard a pin drop," he said. "For a child of your age to be able to hold the entire school in thrall was quite extraordinary. We've always had children here of different abilities, but that was exceptional."

Thank you, Mr. Jefferies, that was really nice.

What do I remember about singing in assembly? I remember kids from the other classes asking why I had such a loud voice.

It's a question I still can't answer.

When I was ten I won a singing scholarship to the Cathedral School, and I said good-bye to St. Mary's. I was sad to leave, but I'd now started singing lessons with Lulu and singing was going to become a very, very big part of my life.

There is another poster in the entrance to St. Mary's. It reads, "Congratulations to Charlotte Church, who left St. Mary's in July 1996 as a fifth-year pupil, having gained a scholarship to the Cathedral School to develop further her outstanding talent. Good luck. We miss you — and remember St. Mary's when you get famous."

How could I forget it?

8

Auntie Caroline

Before I tell you about the Cathedral School, I want to introduce you to my auntie Caroline. Auntie Caroline was the first person to suggest I have singing lessons, and for that, I'll always be grateful.

But there's more to it than that.

Auntie Caroline has always been passionate about singing, and — in a way — it's because of her that I'm the same way. If Auntie Caroline hadn't been a singer, I probably would still have sung, but my stage personality and confidence were inspired by her.

It is also because of Auntie Caroline that I was discovered on TV, but more of that later.

Auntie Caroline is my mum's younger sister, and you can see the resemblance.

They are both small. Caroline is five feet

one, but somehow she's always seemed bigger than that to me.

Auntie Caroline is just as sharp tongued as Mum. They say it like it is, and can they fight! They fight like cats and dogs.

"Always have done and always will," says Auntie.

But no one in my family holds grudges for long.

"Never take your anger to bed," says Mum.

They're both opinionated and fiery, and each of them is always right, which is why they're so close. They talk to each other at least ten times a day.

Auntie Caroline wears skintight jeans and tight tops and cowboy hats, and her hair is cut short and slicked back. When she speaks she growls in a sexy, cabaret singer sort of way, and she's very good at doing her make-up. She does her eyes in dark, smoky colors.

She always looks immaculate.

She and Mum went to the same schools, St. Mary's Primary and Bishop Hannon High School. They were both very good at gymnastics, and Caroline got as far as being picked as a reserve for the Welsh Commonwealth Team. When she was thirteen she gave it up.

"I got scared," she says. "I came off the asymmetric bars and landed on my head, and that was enough to put me off forever."

Instead she started going in for local talent competitions as a dancer — and winning them. She says her motto was "I can do better."

Then she would have to prove it to herself.

When she was fifteen and still at school, she auditioned for a TV show called *Saturday Superstore*. But instead of dancing, at the last minute she decided to sing "I'm Still Standing" by Elton John.

"I had a very low voice," she says. "And people were pleasantly surprised. I didn't get on TV, but I did make the Big Decision. I was going to be a singer.

"That's how it all started for me."

A year later she actually found herself back on *Saturday Superstore* as part of an all-girl dance troupe called Harlem. But she was also beginning to be booked to sing every week at a pub called the Schooner.

This was the beginning of Auntie Caroline's cabaret career.

She left school after, in her own words, "failing my A-Levels miserably," and in the beginning she did all sorts of odd jobs as well as sing.

"Somehow I always managed to cope," she says.

But as soon as she became better known, she began earning enough money to be able to give up the day job. At the Schooner she was billed as "Caroline Cooper, Little Miss Dynamite," and her act lasted forty-five minutes, which was extended to an hour and a half later on.

Mum once suggested that she should be called "the siren of South Wales." I think it was a joke.

You should hear Auntie Caroline sing. You can't believe that such a belting voice can come from such a small person. Auntie Caroline has a voice to bring the house down. She is a professional cabaret singer and sings in pubs and clubs all over South Wales. Sometimes she will drive as far as a hundred miles away to get to a gig on a Saturday night — and then drive back again.

It's *really* hard work.

She sings to backing tapes, and her repertoire is huge. You name it, she can sing it.

She can do chart hits, big show-time numbers, rock, folk, and blues songs. She might start with Madonna's disco version of "Don't Cry for Me, Argentina," then do her impression of Tina Turner. Then she'll finish with a very dramatic "This Is My Life" or "My Heart Will Go On."

She's good at hamming it up. Sometimes,

she says, hamming it up is the *only* way to keep her audience hooked.

"That way at least people will like a couple of the songs," she says.

Auntie Caroline has a wicked sense of humor. She has to. She can be singing her heart out and half the room won't be listening to her. It's tough.

"I used to get upset," she admits. "If you're there giving it everything you've got and someone's reading the newspaper over their beer, it can cut you to shreds. But after I had Elliot I had a different attitude. It didn't matter. I had something more important in my life — my little boy waiting at home for me. So now I just concentrate on the people who are listening."

Auntie Caroline loves being a mum, although when Elliot was eight weeks old she had to go back to the clubs.

As I said earlier, Auntie Caroline lives a few streets away from Nan and Bampy in Canton with her partner, Mark Clucas, who's an electrical fitter, and their five-year-old son, Elliot.

I adore Elliot. Wherever I go, I bring back toys for him — he loves toys from FAO Schwarz in New York. He often stays the night at our house on weekends when Auntie Caroline is out singing. He is only five years old, but he's so serious and so matter-of-fact that, really, he's like a little man.

The thing about my family is they treat the children and the grown-ups in the same way. What I mean is, the children are included in everything.

According to Mum, Elliot is the same way as I was when I was five. He will speak to anyone, grown-ups or children his own age, he isn't shy of singing a song, and as Auntie Caroline says, "His timing's impeccable."

Put on a CD and Elliot will start clapping his hands and miming to the words. He's a great mimic.

Apparently, the first time the family realized that I was going to be a performer was when I was three and a half years old. The family still like to talk about the "first signs."

According to Auntie Caroline, "You were only three years old, approaching your fourth birthday, and it was a winter's afternoon, a Saturday, and James was off playing rugby. Your mum and I and Nan and Bampy took you to the Robin Hood [that's our local pub] for a get-together. Someone put a coin in the jukebox and we heard the voice of Gloria Estefan singing 'Anything for You.'

"Next thing we knew, you had climbed up onto the seat in the booth where we were sitting and you were singing the song as if you'd known it all your life. Word for word. Every note right in perfect pitch and perfect timing.

"Bampy looked at Nan, and I looked at Maria. 'How on earth . . . ?'

" 'It's the radio,' said your mum. 'I can never get her away from it. That song is number one in the charts, and they're playing it all the time. She must have picked it up and memorized it.'

"Then Bampy said very slowly, "Now that is . . . unusual.' "

After that, my family says that there was no stopping me.

A month later, just after my fourth birthday, I did it again.

It was a Sunday afternoon and we were all at the PWD Club on the outskirts of Cardiff to watch Auntie Caroline. Sundays have always been family days, and Auntie Caroline was always grateful for family support.

So there she was, doing her version of Shirley Bassey's "Hey, Big Spender," when, all of a sudden everyone began laughing and clapping.

She had no idea why.

What she didn't know was that I had climbed up on stage behind her and had started dancing in imitation of her. When

Auntie Caroline finally turned round and saw me, she just smiled and kept on singing. She wasn't about to be upstaged by a four-year-old.

Still, as she said later on, "I like my audiences to have a good time, but 'Big Spender' isn't actually a comic number, and I was getting a bit fazed — until I saw you jumping all over the stage behind me."

Then, when the red curtains swished together and Auntie Caroline went off, I stayed behind. Can you believe it?

As though I hadn't had enough, I started singing "Chick, Chick, Chick, Chicken," which was all I could remember at the time.

As Mum likes to point out, "You've always loved an audience."

Dad's got it all on video.

When I was eight and a half I was entered in a local talent show at a club called the Golden Hind. Auntie Caroline rehearsed me on my songs and how to dance on stage. She even made me a spangly gold dress, and I wore bunches in my hair.

Dad videotaped it, so I can actually describe it to you.

I'm singing "Tomorrow" from *Annie* at the top of my lungs. Everyone is clapping, and I'm curtsying. Now I'm singing "On

My Own" from *Les Miserables*.

I've got all of Caroline's dance moves. She was my role model. Secretly I think I wanted to be her.

If I ask her how she feels about my success, she swears it hasn't affected our relationship. Then when other people constantly ask her if she isn't the slightest bit jealous, she says, "I'm not jealous, I'm envious. I'm green with envy. I wish it was me out there getting on TV, traveling the world, and meeting all those incredible people."

I told you Auntie Caroline speaks her mind.

What she means is she's happy for me — like all my family. How does Auntie Caroline think that my success has changed the family?

"Maria can talk about gorgeous hotels they've stayed in around the world," she says.

To be honest, I don't talk about my singing with Auntie Caroline much anymore because I'm away traveling so much and I'm growing up.

I'm fifteen.

I don't want to tell my family everything.

Sometimes when I'm complaining about being tired or having to do more interviews, I know Auntie Caroline must be thinking

I've got nothing to complain about when I've got so much.

She's right.

Anyway, I know that Auntie Caroline's always there for me because she's my auntie.

In the beginning, it was different.

We used to talk about stage fright.

I've never been a very nervous person, not like some performers. I mean, I'm sometimes afraid that I might forget my words when I'm on stage, but as soon as I've started to sing, I'm on such a high that my anxiety disappears.

As Auntie Caroline says, "Once you get up there in the spotlight and sing that first note, your nerves go. We all feel apprehensive, it's natural. You get that cold chill in your tummy, but it will go away if you tell yourself, I'm going to enjoy it. Everything's going to be just fine.

"There's no greater feeling than the adrenaline rush you get when that first wave of applause hits you. It's what being an entertainer is all about. That's why actors and singers do what we do. Whether you're at the London Coliseum singing National Opera or, like me, doing the rounds of smoke-filled clubs across South Wales."

It's really unfair that Auntie Caroline has never had a recording contract. She says she was always in the wrong place at the wrong time. I think she's right.

So much in life is about luck — as well as talent. If she'd been spotted when she was younger, like me, she would definitely have had a record deal. Instead she got married and had Elliot, and she's very happy.

"Most recording companies aren't interested in cabaret," she says. "But I earn my living doing what I love. Singing."

And in our family, Auntie Caroline is a star.

Now I want you to meet Bampy and Nan.

9

Bampy Says, "It's All Rock 'n' Roll, Kid"

Like I said, family is everything to me. At the same time, I can't separate my feelings for my family from my feeling for music. They come from the same place. Music is in my blood, which is why I want you to meet my grand-dad Bampy (or Bampa).

Now don't ask why, where, or how his name began, because it's a mystery. All I know is that it's what I've called him for as long as I can remember.

His real name is Gary Edward Cooper, and he looks like, well, I think he looks like a lovable rogue.

Let me explain.

Bampy isn't tall, nor is he small. He's medium height, with a twinkle in his eye and a bushy mustache. Like I said, he's a plasterer. He's over sixty now and retired. Sort of. He refuses to give it up.

I think of Bampy as mysterious.

I don't know why exactly, but he has an air of mystery about him. He doesn't say a lot, but you get the feeling he knows more than he's letting on. And what he does say somehow means more than you think.

I think of him as a wise old man.

It's Bampy who has taught me about music, about how to feel it and why it's important. I owe him so much.

Bampy taught himself the guitar when he was a boy. By the age of eighteen he was in a band called the Solid Six. He played guitar, and later on he taught himself how to play the tenor saxophone.

"The sax is the sexiest instrument ever invented," he says with a wink. "That sound still sends shivers down my spine."

I don't know about sexy, but I know what he means.

The Solid Six line-up went like this: The singers were called Tony and Vince, the drummer was Mac, Mal was on bass, and Bampy was on rhythm guitar. They spent all their time together, and they had a lot of fun.

Music was Bampy's life.

If he hadn't been musical, I don't know if I'd be musical. What I mean is, music is passed down from generation to generation, isn't it? Bampy calls it "a musical vein that runs through all of us." He's talking about Auntie Caroline, Mum, and me, of course.

Bampy was born in Cardiff in 1938, and he lived in Cardiff until he was eighteen. In 1956 the band bought a van and drove up to London to seek their fortunes.

Right now we're sitting side by side on the couch in the living room. And yes, it's time for another cup of tea.

When I was younger I used to sit on his knee. If I tried to do it now, I would break it. No offense to Bampy, but he is more fragile now than he was, and I'm not a kid anymore.

Okay, Bampy, from the beginning, what happened?

"Well, like I said, we drove up to London in the van. When we got to London we lived in the van for nine months," he says. "We used to park up in Sussex Gardens — or any gardens [like in the film *Notting Hill*], and kip [sleep] in it. Then we moved into rented digs [bedsit] in Paddington and started going round all the clubs, looking for work. Back then the West End was the West End [the only place to go] — and it was all rock 'n' roll, kid. . . ."

This is Bampy's favorite line. It's how he sees life, really. But I'll let him go on.

"We got a few gigs at the Flamingo Club on Wardour Street [in Soho] and the Contemporary Club in Mayfair. The clubs were jumping. People used to dress up in those days, and everyone knew how to dance properly, like. We used to play 'The Twist,' and if the kids couldn't stand up because there wasn't space, they would do the hand-jive in their seats.

"We got an agent, then we got signed up by Oriel Records, but our timing wasn't good. The Beatles happened right after us, and they were an impact band. The new stuff had started. Rock 'n' roll was finished. Even so, we did a record called 'The Method,' which was a dance record. And another record called 'The Franz Liszt Twist' was a kind of jazzed-up version of a piece of Liszt's called 'Liebestraum,' and it went to number three in Holland and number four in Australia.

"We thought we'd made the big time."

But Bampy's band wasn't earning a proper living.

And as Bampy says, "You can't live out of a van forever." Anyway, by this point Bampy had been courting Nan, whose real name is Maureen, for six years. She'd had enough of all his touring. She wanted him to come back to Cardiff and settle down.

Nan and Bampy met in Cardiff when Nan

was sixteen. They met at a dance in a hall called the Sophia Gardens on a Saturday night.

What were Bampa's first impressions of Nan?

He smiles. "Oh, she was a delightful girl. Two years younger than me, with a lovely nature and a smile to match. We found we had a lot in common. We liked music and films. And her knowledge of films put me to shame. She loved all the big fifties film stars. Cary Grant, Gary Cooper . . ."

That's Bampy's little joke, by the way.

"I remember taking her down to the Moon Club, and that was the first time I saw girls drinking out of bottles."

Nan's joined us. She's joined us in the living room on the other couch. She knows exactly what Bampy's talking about.

"Yes, I was the first rocker to play in the Moon Club. Before that they only had a dance band. . . ."

That was Bampy being wistful again.

"I remember I was wearing a black dress and pearls. It was the early sixties, and it was the days when girls were burning their bras and wearing jeans," says Nan.

"I asked you what you wanted to drink."

"I said vodka and lime."

"And I said I don't think they have glasses

here, only Newcastle bitter [beer] in bottles."

"And I said I am *not* going to drink beer out of a bottle."

"But what happened when Bampy moved to London with the band, Nan?" I ask. "Did you go up to London to see him?"

"Oh yes. Every other Friday night after work, I'd catch the train up to London and your granddad would come and pick me up. The band had rented a house just outside of London in Surrey, and a lot of weekends they were playing in the U.S. Air Force camps. So I'd go along to the gigs."

"And Bampy, tell us again about Israel."

"I went, too," says Nan. "Although the band wasn't called the Solid Six anymore. It was called the Gary Edwards Combo."

Bampy's gone off to get his photograph album.

"It was spring 1963, and your nan and I'd just got married. Here's the band," he says. He's pointing to a black-and-white photograph of four men in suits with guitar cases in their hands. Here's another photograph of a long line of people waiting to get into a nightclub.

"Our fans," says Bampy. "We were in Israel for three months. We were big in Israel. We had all the government dignitaries —

94

and the Prime Minister — jiving in their seats. How about that?"

Now they're laughing.

Nan has a husky smoker's laugh. But I think their laughter can sometimes sound the same. It's not high or low, just relaxed. It's funny how people who have been married for a long time grow alike. Nan and Bampy have been married for almost forty years. In public Nan is the authority, but Bampy has her wrapped around his little finger. She cooks for him and irons his shirts. She does everything for him. They adore each other.

But secretly.

They never show their affection openly. Sometimes Bampy tries to, but Nan always brushes him off. Then she'll shout at him, but that's just the way it is between them.

I love listening to them, but back to the story.

I lived with Mum at Nan and Bampy's house until I was four and a half. Later, when I was at St. Mary's, I would go round to their house every day after school and Bampy would take me to the park. For tea, we would get fish and chips, and Bampy would always buy me a box of Jelly Tots, which are like jelly beans dusted in sugar. They were my favorite sweets when I was younger.

And Bampy would always sing me songs, all sorts of songs. Most of them old rock 'n' roll hits from the fifties. Musically, Bampy has been a huge source of inspiration. He's always whistling a tune or beating out a rhythm on the arm of a chair. But Nan won't let him play his records in the house too often because she likes her quiet — and her classical music.

Nan loves Puccini.

Bampy says he realized early on that I was musical and his encouragement was only natural.

"I can still picture you on my knee singing away like the fury," he says. "Sometimes we'd catch you singing in front of the mirror with a hairbrush as a microphone. But it wasn't until you were eight or nine that we realized your potential. You were hitting notes which gave me goose bumps. You were born with perfect pitch."

Most of all, Bampy taught me about the emotion of singing. Emotion should never be left out because it's the most important thing.

Bampy's second piece of advice, which I still think about when I'm performing, is that every song tells a story and everyone loves a good story.

"Even Humpty-Dumpty tells a story," he says. "Just not a very long one. Whatever the story is, it has to be told with conviction that will capture the audience's attention and hold it.

"You live every note you sing. Go for the tears and the laughter. Like with 'Danny Boy,' which is a traditional Irish song and a lament. It's a song that has been sung so many ways, but it's the interpretation that's different.

"That's the advice I gave your auntie Caroline when she first set foot on stage, and that's what I'm telling you. Finish your words, speak properly, and it'll give you natural breathing. Good diction is vital."

Bampy always says Nat King Cole had the best phrasing of anyone in the whole world — ever. Frank Sinatra and Barbra Streisand, too.

I know what Bampy means.

I'm not a big fan of theirs, but I have to agree with Bampy that when Frank Sinatra sings a song, he makes it his own. It's magical and special and normal all at the same time.

Which reminds me of Bampy's other words of wisdom.

"Present yourself properly, but be yourself and be your natural self. And always smile."

Which is what I try to do.

97

Now when I'm performing — in Cardiff or London or Los Angeles — it means a lot to me to have the family in the audience, particularly Bampy.

When they're there I try much harder.

I try to sing better for them than I did for the Pope or the President — or anyone.

My family is everything to me.

Now here's Nan.

10
Nan

Nan is the rock of the family. She's calm most of the time, but she can be stern when she needs to be. When you meet Nan you understand where Auntie Caroline and Mum come from and where they get their toughness from — and I mean that in a good way.

Nan can worry sometimes.

"I don't like reading about you in the newspapers," she says. "It's strange."

I know it is.

"I don't like it when people I meet when I'm out at the shops ask me questions about you," she says. "People think because you're famous, you're different. You're not. At home you're just an ordinary fifteen-year-old girl."

My family keep my feet firmly on the ground. And I know that Nan is happy for me and that she wants me to be happy, that's all.

"I'm always here if you need me," she says. "I'm always ready to give you a hug. Oh, you're such a huggy child."

Then I'll hug her.

Nan has a lovely smell. She smells clean and warm. She has beautiful skin and rosy cheeks and silver hair and a *really* big smile. She's shorter than Bampy, but she's largish — in a comfortable way. She always looks nice. She wears layered clothes, she likes white and black, and she's very elegant. She wears big gemmy jewelry and pearls in her ears. She doesn't look grandmotherly, she looks motherly.

What I mean is, she wears what a woman in her forties might wear.

She loves going shopping — especially when the sales are on. She loves getting dressed up on a Saturday night and going out with her best friend, Maureen. They go to their favorite club and have a drink and tell stories and get silly.

Nan was born and brought up in Cardiff.

Nan's favorite subjects at school were history and English, and even now she loves a good book. She loves mysteries and romances and biographies. She's just finished Charlie Chaplin's biography, and before that she was reading David Niven's biography. She likes reading about the film stars who were big when she was a girl.

"My dad loved showbiz, and so do I," she says.

Nan doesn't go to the cinema anymore because she doesn't like modern films.

"I loved the musicals like *Guys and Dolls* and the epics like *Ben-Hur*," she says. "They don't make them like that anymore."

When Nan left school she went to work as a clerk at Roath Radio Company.

When she had Auntie Caroline and Mum, she gave up her job to look after them. When Auntie Caroline was old enough to start school, Nan got a job serving lunches in the cafeteria of a local elementary school. She worked there for twenty-five years.

But the family always comes first with Nan.

"Family is the *only* thing that's important," she says.

She's a devout Catholic. She says she has kept her faith because that's what her mother wanted. Nan goes to St. Mary's Catholic Church every Sunday without fail and prays for all of us.

When I was seven I took Holy Communion at St. Mary's Church, and I had to learn the Lord's Prayer, and I wore a white dress.

I still pray.

I believe that if there's something you really want to change, you can change it by praying hard enough.

Mum prays a lot. If she's lost something, she will pray to St. Anthony, and because of her prayers she will find whatever she has lost. That's what she thinks, anyway.

I know Nan would like it if I went to church more often. I do believe in God. Right now I'm really interested in exploring ancient religions like Hinduism. Reincarnation and karma are ideas that really fascinate me, and I want to find out more.

What Nan and I both agree on is that the most important thing is to believe in something.

I'm at Nan's house right now.

Nan's house is home, and when I'm here there's nowhere else I'd rather be.

As Mum says, "It's more than a second home, it's on par with our first home."

Mum *still* sometimes spends the night here at Nan's.

"I'll often say to James, 'Oh, I'm going round to my mum's tonight,'" says Mum. "And I'll stay the night — and Caroline does the same. Our bedrooms are still the same, with our single beds from when we were girls. Sometimes if there's three of us because you're here [she means me], we'll double up and share a bed."

We're sitting in Nan's living room, which is my favorite room.

It looks exactly the way it did when Mum and Auntie Caroline were kids, although the wallpaper has been redone and the couches have been replaced. When I'm here, I always think about how much has happened in this room. Happy moments and sad moments and all the moments before I was born.

The carpet is red and the walls are cream and the couch is dark brown. There are photographs of the family on the walls. There's one of Caroline when she was about twenty-four. One of me when I was seven or eight. There are some of Mum and Dad's wedding with me and my cousin Nadine and Auntie Caroline as bridesmaids.

Nan loves being a grandma. She baby-sits for Elliot when Auntie Caroline is off singing. She loves fussing over us and making sure we've got enough to eat. She loves it when we're all here at her house and she can cook a big stew with dumplings or shepherd's pie or pancakes.

She's a fabulous cook. Her dishes are simple but ever so tasty. Every Sunday lunchtime we'll either go to her house or Auntie Caroline's house for roast lamb or roast beef. That way we always get to see each other.

Nan likes cider or a nice glass of wine or,

best of all, a glass of champagne.

And here she is sitting on the couch next to me with her feet up.

Good.

Nan has worked hard all of her life, and I want her to sit back and enjoy life a bit more. One of the best things about my career is that it helps to treat Nan and the rest of the family. It makes me happy to be able to take her to places she has never visited before. To give something back to her.

Nan loved her trip to Rome.

"I hadn't been abroad since your grand-dad sent me a plane ticket to go and join him in Israel in 1963," she says. "I adored Rome. I have to say I was really disappointed that I couldn't meet the Pope, but going to the Vatican and seeing inside St. Peter's and going to the dinner with all the cardinals after your concert was wonderful."

Then she came to Los Angeles with Bampy to see me play at the Hollywood Bowl. Nan loved it there.

"It was just like in the films," she says, laughing. "What with the trip to Rome and then Los Angeles, I've done more traveling in the past two years than I've done all my life."

But I want to know what it was like when she was young.

"Tell me about Bampy when you first met him," I say. "What was he like?"

I watch her eyes crinkle up.

"What I liked about him was he was a great rock 'n' roll dancer. We went dancing every single night, and once we were on the dance floor there was no stopping us."

They don't rock 'n' roll anymore because Nan's got asthma.

But she's smiling because she's remembering, and I feel happy for her.

"Now, who wants a cup of tea?" she says.

"I do, but you stay there, Nan," I tell her. "I'll make it."

11

Singing with Lulu

Now that you've met the family, I'd like you to meet another really important person, someone I've spent so much time with over the past five years that, really, she's family, too: Lulu, my singing teacher.

Lulu's real name is Louise Ryan, but everyone calls her Lulu.

She says it's a friendship thing and a Welsh thing, and I think she's probably right. Like I said, the Welsh are very friendly, and everyone's names get shortened.

Lulu's in her mid-thirties, and to me she looks like an opera singer. What I mean is, she's rounded in the way opera singers are. She has slightly reddish hair, which she curls and wears on top of her head with bits dangling down. She has almond-shaped eyes and really long eyelashes, and like my Mum, Auntie Caroline, and me, Lulu loves her makeup. You'll never see Lulu without lipstick and mascara on.

Everything about Lulu is about her voice.

First of all, there's her posture. You have to keep your spine straight when you sing, and Lulu has a very straight back. Then there's the way she uses her hands all the time to emphasize what she's saying. And of course, there's the way she speaks. Lulu's not from Wales, she's originally from the south coast of England, although you can't really place her by her accent.

Lulu speaks very well. She has *very* good diction, she never slurs her words, and her singing voice is fabulous. She's a soprano like me, and she trained as a classical singer.

More about that later on.

I'll tell you about how Lulu and I met. But first I'll tell you about her house.

The area of Cardiff that Lulu lives in is called Roath. It's closer to the city center than Llandaff or Canton. The houses are red brick and there are lots of trees and it's close to the university, so a lot of students live here. All the houses on Lulu's street are painted different colors. Lulu's house is brick colored, with a blue front door.

I'm here for my lesson.

I can hear faraway barking getting louder and louder. Lulu's two dogs are racing to get to the door. It's always the same way.

"Shut up, Piglet, it's not for you."

That's Lulu trying to get the dogs out of the way. She opens the door.

"Hi, Lulu."

"Hi there. Come in."

The dogs scamper after me, barking excitedly. Piglet (you know — from *Winnie-the-Pooh*) is a West Highland white terrier, and Penny is a white cairn. They know me.

Well, they should after five years.

Off the hallway on the right is Lulu's lounge, which is where she teaches. It's a lovely, warm room with yellow and blue walls and pictures of sunflowers and pears in brightly colored frames.

It's a room with loads of character, just like Lulu.

At the far end of the room there are shelves stacked with music books. Lulu has classical music and the scores to every musical you can think of, from *Annie* to *Requiem* by Andrew Lloyd Webber, which is where the song "Pie Jesu" comes from.

There is a window next to the piano that looks out onto a yard and a statue of a dog barking at the moon. Next to the window is an upright piano and a music stand. This is the corner of the room where I stand and sing. I sing scales and I rehearse my songs just like all the other students Lulu teaches.

Can you imagine if all the children and grown-ups Lulu has taught — and she has been teaching in this house for ten years — tried to fit into this room?

What a squash.

Although, come to think of it, I don't think we'd fit. Lulu's students come in all shapes and sizes. What I mean is, she teaches a lot of very different people.

Lulu says, "It's rare to find someone who can't sing, and all my students have something to offer. As long as they're getting satisfaction and improving each week, it's satisfying for me and it's satisfying for them. I have school kids and college students and housewives. You know the way housewives go the hairdresser's once a week for a social thing? Well, they come here instead — just for a laugh."

We're sitting on Lulu's blue couch with lots of cushions on it. Penny and Piglet are curled up between us. Lulu has given me a glass of my favorite Ribena (blackcurrant cordial with water), and she's drinking coffee.

Here's my first question.

"How did you meet Mum?"

"I met your auntie Caroline first. One night I went out with some friends to hear the cabaret. Your auntie Caroline was singing. She was known as being one of the best singers around — and still is, for that matter.

"We got talking. She said she might come and do a few lessons because she'd had a few problems with her voice, like most singers, and we exchanged telephone numbers.

"Then, it might have been six or seven years later, a long time, anyway, I got a phone call one day — completely out of the blue.

" 'I'm Caroline's sister and I've got a daughter and I'd like her to do some singing lessons,' she said.

"It was Maria. At Caroline's suggestion, Maria wanted you to have some lessons because she was worried you might damage your voice in the same way that Caroline, who was self-taught, had damaged her voice."

"What was I like when you first met me?"

Lulu is laughing. She has a very loud and fast laugh. It's a staccato laugh — like a witch or a machine gun.

"Oh, you just came bounding in and I thought, I've got a right one here."

"Nothing's changed, then."

"No. You were only nine years old, but you were so confident, saying hello to the dogs. Most kids your age are hiding behind their parents. But because you were so used to getting up on stage and singing with Caroline, you weren't scared at all. I thought it was great."

"I remember we started off doing scales."

"Yes. I got you over there in the corner and we started doing scales, la la la la la la la la, and you just kept going up and up and up.

"That was my first surprise. Then I asked if you wanted to sing a song. And, no surprise here, you said you wanted to sing 'Tomorrow' from *Annie,* which secretly is my pet hate. All the little girls want to sing it. They put on a precocious American accent and start wailing with these screaming voices until their necks expand. But I thought, I'll let you sing it so that I can see what your personality's like."

"I loved that song."

"Have I ever let you sing it again?"

"Er . . . no."

"You started singing, and out came this voice that was so clean and pure and well in tune and well balanced and, well, let's just say the proverbial jaw hit the floor."

I think what Lulu's trying to say is that she was a bit surprised by my voice.

"That's the understatement of the century. What happened was Maria was sitting in that armchair, and I turned to her, so that you couldn't see me, and I went like this. . . ."

Lulu's opened her mouth as far as it will go.

"I was flabbergasted."

So there you have my first lesson with Lulu.

After that I started coming once a week for half an hour. The older I got, the longer my lessons became. By the age of eleven, I was singing with Lulu for an hour. Now when I'm preparing for a concert, we have two-hour-long lessons.

I'll let Lulu carry on.

"Your mum was a trained musician on the guitar, and she knew the discipline involved in taking up an instrument seriously, and she wanted you to do exams and enter into the competitions and festivals and Eisteddfod [a Welsh festival that covers all the arts and is a huge institution]."

"I can still remember the songs you taught me in the beginning. I sang 'Walking in the Air' from *The Snowman*."

"Yes. Although 'Pie Jesu' came pretty soon afterward because I wanted you to enjoy singing all those high notes. That's why I got you into the classical stuff straightaway."

Lulu started singing lessons herself when she was twelve years old.

She says that she'd always sung in her school choirs, and when she was put in for competitions, she won them. No one in her family knew where her musical ability came from. Her father was a sailor and her mother was a teacher, but they supported her gift. When she came to Cardiff to audition for a place at the Welsh College of Music and Drama, she fell in love with the people, the trees, the sky, and the city.

Back to Lulu.

"I did a three-year diploma in performing and postgraduate studies. At the end of it, I decided to teach. I'd wanted to teach ever since I was a kid, and I adore it. I love teaching new pieces and watching my students progress. It gives me huge satisfaction. I get to play the piano and sing every day. I've had such a great time."

If I had to describe Lulu's kind of teaching, I'd say it was fun.

"Lulu, how would you describe your teaching?"

Lulu laughs. "Unconventional, productive, and *fun.*"

I told you.

"I never did a teaching degree, but I did one in performing, and that's the difference. I teach all the academic stuff and get my students through their exams, but I treat each of my students as individuals. I try to ascertain what will work for them and what they need to know.

"With you, every time I had taught you one thing, you could hardly wait to get on to the next one. There I was, trying to behave like the textbook singing teacher who didn't want to overwork a ten-year-old. Meanwhile, I could see that you were so enthusiastic, if I didn't show you how to get the sound you wanted — you would have screamed your head off."

I think Lulu's right. All I know is that I've always wanted to learn more and, I suppose, improve on what I can already do.

I think the next thing to tell you about is Lulu's rules. I wouldn't be doing what I'm doing today if it wasn't for Lulu *or* her rules.

The most important thing to learn about singing is breathing.

Lulu is really strict about standing up straight — aren't you, Lulu?

"Absolutely. Deportment is very important. I always stand in front of my students — as I did with you — and show them how to stand. We do ballerina poses. The students always think they're very funny.

"You have to keep the pelvis nice and square and breathe into the diaphragm, which is just below the chest, and not breathe *into* the chest. That's why I get my students to put their hands on their ribs to see if their rib cages expand properly. It will increase the more properly they breathe.

When you first came to me you had a chest voice. That was the first mistake. That was why, even though you could belt out your songs, you only had a little bit of air to work with."

"Okay, so after breathing, what came next? I can't remember."

"You got the breathing no problem. What was amazing was then you wanted to know how to get your voice from your neck to the front of your face. This is what classically trained singers are taught to do — to sing and talk from their cheekbones. I have students twice your age who can't hear the difference. And you were all of ten and a half.

"So I showed you how us oldies do it — and you just did it. You always were a very good mimic, which is another good quality a singer needs to have. And now you could make what we call a 'round' sound instead of an 'airy' sound."

"Then what?"

"Then when you were eleven, you asked me, 'How do I keep my breath there?' I couldn't believe it. You were tiny. You hardly knew where your big toe was, let alone your lower abdomen. Most teachers say you shouldn't teach students about the lower abdomen and controlling the breath from the lower abdomen until they're at least sixteen years old. But I knew you would get frustrated if I didn't show you."

"I must have driven you mad."

"You said, 'Show me, show me,' and I was looking at you, smiling, thinking you're so advanced for your years, you're so enthusiastic, you're bound to get it. So I said, 'Well, you see that panel down there, that's what you need to *lift* to give yourself the strength.'

"Then I explained that it feels the same as barking, or coughing, or saying 'Ho ho ho' like Santa Claus. It's like a heaving motion. Almost like throwing up. It comes from right down there below your tummy.

"Well, by Jove, you got it."

Now we're laughing.

It's funny to think of me learning what now seems like the most natural thing in the world. I can't remember the actual moment I learned how to control my voice, but it was after this that everything else happened. Lulu says it was the turning point.

Lulu also jumps to my defense about the critics who say I'm too young to be singing as a soprano.

"They don't know you and how quickly you've matured. From the age of ten to thirteen, the extent to which your voice improved in terms of control and the size was huge," she says. "They say your body is too young, but if your brain's not too young, then your body is certainly not too young. If you had been a normal, average ten- or eleven-year-old kid, then I wouldn't have taught you how to do the breathing. That said, you're *still* not ready for everything. You are only fourteen. Your voice will continue to improve."

Lulu always says that it was her experience of being told she *couldn't* sing what she wanted to sing when she was young that has influenced the way she teaches now.

I'll let Lulu explain.

"From my experience, one of the worst things you can do is say no. When I was at school I wanted to be in Oliver, which the boys' school was doing up the road. My singing teacher and my parents said I couldn't because it would ruin my classically trained voice.

"When I was at college I sang with a forty-piece jazz band. I absolutely loved it, but I was told off by the head of vocal studies, again, because I was going to ruin my classical voice. I was forbidden to do it.

"You can advise people obviously if you think they're going to damage their voice, but you should never, ever, say, 'No, you *cannot* do that.' "

I always trust Lulu's advice.

When I was still nine, Lulu put me in for my first official public appearance.

It was at an Eisteddfod — the big cultural festival that takes place once a year in Cardiff.

"It will be a good sounding board for you," was how Lulu put it.

The Eisteddfod was held in a big hall. I sang "Walking in the Air," and I won.

That was the first live concert that Lulu rehearsed me for. Since then, as well as being in the recording studio for all three of my albums, Lulu has traveled the world with me. She has been with me to Sweden, Japan, America, and Israel.

When we're traveling, she gives me my daily singing lessons. When I'm performing, I like having Lulu with me because if I can't work out where I've gone wrong, Lulu can. Lulu knows every breath I should take *and* where to take it. She encourages me. She makes me feel comfortable, and she reminds me of anything and everything I might have forgotten.

If I'm feeling tired before a concert, I jump up and down to get my adrenaline pumping and my breath flowing faster. Another Lulu trick.

She was at my first showcase in New York

where I sang four songs from my first album for the American press. It was a really big day.

Here's Lulu.

"I'm there at the showcases so that when you're warming up during rehearsal and the producer comes running up and says, 'What's wrong?' I can say, 'Calm down. If she's not brilliant in rehearsal, it means she's going to be fantastic in the performance.' And you are."

Lulu is a calming influence. She says she absorbs my excess energy and my nerves, and she does.

And like Bampy, Lulu has also taught me about emotion. As she says, what a singer does, when they sing live, anyway, is bare their soul to people *and* convince the audience that they mean it.

And the secret to good singing?

Happiness.

As Lulu says, "If there's anything wrong with any part of the body, it's going to affect the singing. When a person is stressed or tense or in pain, the voice is hard to get out."

Then she will look at me and say, "So you're happy, right? Because that's why your voice is working so well."

Right.

Lulu says, "Singing live is what it's all

about," and I agree. Singing to an audience, particularly in the open air, is magical.

Lulu gets a bit gushy here.

"There are certain songs you sing that still, even now, make my heart stop. They tend to be the Irish songs — probably because I'm half Irish — like 'Danny Boy' or 'She Moved Through the Fair.' And because I hear you so often, I take your abilities for granted. Then when I see a new audience's reaction to you in a live concert, I'm always amazed at how shocked they are at how good you are."

Lulu and I don't talk about the future of my singing, but I know that Lulu thinks the same thing as me.

The next thing is going to be to find the right repertoire to suit whatever changes I'm going to make with the direction of my music.

As Lulu says, "Whatever you're singing, you've just got to have a good time. Then the audience will love you."

12

My Bedroom

Now before I go on with my story, I want to stop and give you a guided tour of my favorite place, my bedroom. This is where I'm telling you most of my story from.

So let me show you round.

Last summer we moved house.

The part of Cardiff we've moved to is called Whitchurch. It's not far from Llandaff or Canton, it's on the same side of town, and it's just as green. It's a new house. We're the first to live in it, which means it doesn't have ghosts. Only joking. It's just that we reckon my friend Abby's house is haunted, although that's another story.

Why did we move?

We ran out of space at our old house in Llandaff. Our old house is a small terrace house, which suited us fine when I was younger and I wasn't singing. But now that I have *so* many stage clothes, they don't fit in my closet. They were taking up most of the guest room.

We also lived next door to a school. The kids knew that I lived next door. And although I'll always sign an autograph if someone asks me and I'll always say hello to people who want to talk to me, kids were ringing the doorbell at seven o'clock in the morning.

It drove Dad mad.

"No, you *cannot* have her autograph. Do you know what time it is?!" he would explode.

He hadn't even had his first cup of tea.

The new house, or our dream house, as we call it, is detached. It's surrounded by a wall and a security camera. I don't want to make it sound worse than it is, but I have had a few funny people follow me home. One man told me that I was a messenger from God and that he had come to collect a message from me.

To be on the safe side, we think it's better to be able to see who is ringing the bell.

The new house is a big investment, but I don't think we'll be moving out of here in a hurry. It's wicked. The living room is so huge that there's room for all the family to come round — and their families, too. The dining room can seat at least eight people. And there's a music room with a piano so that Lulu can come and teach me and enough wall space in the dining room to hang all my framed records from Sony.

Best of all — we've put in a swimming pool and a sauna so that we can all stay fit. I love swimming. It's my favorite exercise, and since Dad injured his back playing rugby, it's the only exercise he can do. As for Mum, she's pretty good at the breaststroke.

But my bedroom is my favorite room.

Like I said before, it's soundproofed, which means that when my best friends, Abby, Kim, and Jo, whom you will meet later on, sleep over and we're up all night gossiping, Mum and Dad won't know (although they can normally tell by the dazed looks on our faces the next morning when Dad's making breakfast and asking who wants bacon — and no one answers).

My bedroom's floor is hardwood, and the walls are cream. I like the simple look. But I also wanted my bedroom to have a theme. Since Eygptian was impossible — where was I going to find a bed with hieroglyphics? — I decided to go for a Chinese look. I wanted something ethnic and a little bit exotic, and I love Chinese films.

I've put twenty-five candle holders from a

Chinese shop, Neal Street East, in London all over the room. I've put up framed pictures of Chinese art with Chinese writing around them. I've got a low table made out of ebony, or something like it, in the middle of the room, and around it are piles of cream and red cushions.

Then there's a carved chest of drawers that looks like an antique, though it isn't, *and* Chinese lanterns with writing on them hanging from the ceiling.

I feel like I'm in my own Chinese movie.

So you know how much my tastes have changed, the walls of my old bedroom were yellow, orange, green, and blue. The carpet was yellow, and the curtains were flowery orange and green. Everything was bright. I even had an inflatable red chair in the corner and all over my bed and the floor and in the inflatable chair were hundreds, and I'm not exaggerating, of cuddly toys.

I think everyone knows how much I loved cuddly toys.

Everywhere I went, I was given cuddly toys. Sometimes I used to take them on stage with me and introduce them to the audience before I sang.

I've given some of them away. I gave some to a children's hospital here in Cardiff because they meant more to the children than they did to me. I've kept a few, my favorites. The wild ones. I've still got Puma and Penguin and Gorilla and my best friend, Bernard, a *huge* dog, who lies at the end of my bed. When I'm feeling lazy I lie on top of him. He has floppy ears.

What are the most important things in my room?

Definitely the two sofa beds that my friends sleep on at weekends. Then there's all my makeup that, right now, is on top of my chest of drawers. My favorites at the moment are Poppy lip gloss called Shine and black Maybelline mascara.

I have to confess, I adore shoes.

I have at least twenty pairs. If I had to try to summarize what I like, I'd say that I like high shoes. I like wedge heels. I like classy shoes that make your feet look thin. At the moment I'm U.K. size five, I think that's a U.S. seven, but my feet are still growing.

Some of my shoes I've picked up on my travels. I've got a pair of strappy sandals from Singapore that cost nothing, and I love them to death. I love my pink Shelley's sneakers with a wedge heel that look like Buffalo shoes, like the ones the Spice Girls used to wear. I've got a pair of pink Miu Miu sandals with strings that wrap around your ankles that I bought for one of my concerts.

I've got a pair of lilac sandals.

Oh, and my favorite shoes at the moment are a pair of mules with diamanté toes and wooden heels. They are lush, which means gorgeous.

And I love bags. I've got a red satin Chinese bag that looks fab with everything in my room. Oh, and here's my pink ostrich feather boa that I wrap around my neck when I *really* want to dress up.

I'm a clothesaholic. Inside my closet is a load of different stuff. My favorite clothes for every day are baggy pants, combat style, that fall low on the hips. I wear them with belly tops, snug Ts that show your belly.

My friend Kim wants to have her belly button pierced. I'm not into piercing.

My dungarees are so comfy, I could wear them all the time. On stage I sometimes wear trouser suits made by the English designer Karen Millen. I own lots of pink because people give me pink accessories and clothes because they think I'm girly. I'm not . . . well, not really. I mean, I own only three skirts and I never wear them. I wear long skirts and dresses on stage, but as soon as I'm off the stage I'm straight back into my pants.

How do I decide what to wear to concerts?

I've got two great stylists, one in the United

Kingdom and one in America. If it's an open-air concert, we'll look at the weather. If it's close to Christmas, we can be more over the top, which is fun. Lots of red and sequins and glitter.

Usually what happens is I take a choice of outfits with me. When we're all in my dressing room, Mum will come up with one idea, Terry Kenny (who's a sweetie and you haven't met yet) will suggest something else. I'll want to wear something completely different. We'll have a huge argument, and in the end we'll decide.

Funny how it always works like that.

The other great thing about what I do is that I sometimes get to keep the clothes that I've worn on photo shoots.

When I go into town I'll sometimes put on my sunglasses. I'm really into glasses.

What else is there to tell you about my room?

I've got a TV in my room, but I never watch it, although I still love *The Jerry Springer Show* and I love MTV.

When I have sleep-overs with my friends, we just hang out and chat and eat candy. Our favorite candies are strawberry laces, wine gums, Harabos, and cola candies.

We used to watch movies. We were all really into Stephen Dorff. He was so cool as the vampire in *Blade*. I loved *Girl, Interrupted* with Angelina Jolie. She's a fabulous actress. She has this magnetic personality, and I think Nicole Kidman is amazing to look at, and I loved her movie *Practical Magic*. I like movies with good actors and a great plot.

When I was really young, I loved *Mary Poppins*. I think it was because I wanted to fly.

Now when I'm alone in my room, I listen to music and talk on my phone to my friends.

I used to love playing computer games. My favorite was Tekken 3.

Not anymore.

Right now I've got the stereo on, and I'm listening to my favorite album, Craig David's *Born to Do It*. Robbie's new album. He's lush *and* he can sing. He's got a fabulous voice. My friends love the Backstreet Boys. I think they're okay.

I'm really into R 'n' B at the moment. I love Lauryn Hill and Destiny's Child and Pink and Kelis. I also love singers with great voices. I love Cerys Matthews from Catatonia, who is (of course) Welsh, and Alanis Morissette and the Corrs.

I used to like the Spice Girls, but now I like All Saints. I used to have posters of Ricky Martin and Robbie Williams on my wall, but now that I've met them, and I'm older, there's *no* way I'd have pictures of them.

I've got a few photographs of me with different famous people on a shelf on the wall. Here I am with Tom Jones and George Michael. Here I am shaking hands with the Pope and with President Clinton.

I've met some amazing people.

Who would I meet if I was allowed to pick anyone in the whole wide world?

Let me see.

Alanis Morissette, because she tells it like it is. Craig David and Madonna and Jill Scott. I'd like to meet Angelina Jolie and Nicole Kidman to talk about acting.

Oh, and what about including people from the past?

In that case, I'd like to meet Jesus and the Virgin Mary and Mary Magdalene and Cleopatra and Mark Antony and Caesar and Octavian (or Augustus, as he's better known), and Elvis Presley and Frank Sinatra and Princess Diana and Judy Garland.

Oh, I could go on and on.

So let's talk about really important people — my friends.

I don't have photographs of them on my walls because I keep them in my purse. We take photographs in the passport photo booths in town. You know the machines that take head shots of one person at a time? Well, what we do is cram all four of us inside so that our faces are squashed together, and we're normally hysterical with laughter and pulling faces by the time the flash goes off.

At school we write notes to each other.

Outside school we text message each other on our mobile phones. Here's one from Naomi:

Did you buy any CDs today? TB

TB means text back, so I had better quickly text back and tell her how fabulous the Craig David CD is.

In school mobile phones are banned. That's why we write notes. I keep them here in my bedside drawer, and when I go away I take them with me and read them because they make me laugh, and they make me think of them.

Here's one from Emily. She's obsessed with Ewan McGregor, and she always speaks with a Scottish accent:

Alright Churchy? — I'm called Churchy as well as Charl and Chee-Chee — *I don't know if you're expecting a note back but I'll send one anyway because I'm bored, naturally. I've just heard that Mrs. Fitz just had a fit. Ha Ha. Sorry about my little joke. If I were you I would take the opportunity to run, run like the wind, not that I want you to go away. I have a piano exam on Monday. I'm so bored. HELP! Where have you been recently? Tell me something I don't know. Oh well, nice talking to you. Bye.*

I read all the magazines I can get my hands on.

Here on my bed, I've got *Teen People*, *Looks*, and the *Top of the Pops* magazines with me at the moment. Britney Spears is on the cover of *Looks*. She's pretty, but Kate Moss is stunning. Here's Christina Ricci, she's stunning, too. Madonna is fab and so clever. Martine McCutcheon is beautiful. We met her and she has a really pretty face.

Gwyneth Paltrow would probably fall over if you blew on her. She's all right, though.

I love reading books, although I do most of my reading on planes, not here in my bedroom.

My favorite book? (Besides *Harry Potter*, of course.)

It has to be *The Memoirs of Cleopatra; A Novel* by Margaret George. It's a thousand pages long. It took me two months to read.

When I got to the end, I read it again. When I'm eighteen I want to travel to Eygpt and see the Pyramids. I don't know why, but I'm fascinated by ancient civilizations. It's mainly to do with Cleopatra and Africa, which I think of as mysterious and magical.

I wrote a screenplay at school recently. It was about the first time Cleopatra and Caesar met. What happened, if you don't know the story, was that Cleopatra was overthrown by her brother and sister and fled to the desert. The guards wouldn't let her back into the palace. But Caesar had arrived to stay at the palace, and she decided that she would charm him into putting her back on the throne.

She wrapped herself up in a rug, and a carpet merchant carried her through the gates of the palace, saying that he had a gift for Caesar. When he put the rug on the floor, Cleopatra rolled out. . . .

"Charlotte!"

Mum's calling me. Time for dinner.

13

I'm Discovered

When I was growing up, Auntie Caroline always encouraged me to sing.

But Auntie Caroline played another, and very important, role in my career, not that we knew it at the time. It's actually thanks to Auntie Caroline that I got on TV in the first place.

And it was because of that first appearance on TV that everything else happened. Because of going on *Richard and Judy*, I was invited to go on *The Big, Big Talent Show*. Because I was on the *The Big, Big Talent Show*, all sorts of agents and managers approached me, and in the space of five months — which everyone says isn't a very long time — I ended up meeting Paul Burger from Sony Music and was given a record deal.

But — let's start at the beginning, shall we.

January 10, 1997. I was on Christmas break.

All the other schools in Cardiff had already gone back for spring term, but Cathedral School gave us an extra week of holiday. Mum was back at work, and Auntie Caroline was looking after me.

Breakfast time, and we were eating our toast and drinking our tea and watching the breakfast TV show *Richard and Judy* (it's sort of like *Live with Regis and Kathie Lee*), just like we always did.

But on this particular morning, Richard and Judy were asking "talented kids" to call in if they had something special to say — or sing.

"Go on. Let's do it," said Auntie Caroline.

Before I knew it, Auntie Caroline had dialed the call-in number flashing on the TV screen, and we were put on hold. Then, without giving me time to think, I had the telephone in my hand, I was asked my name, asked what I was going to sing — and then I sang it.

What did I sing?

"Pie Jesu," of course, because, like Lulu says, it's a good song for showing off my soprano voice.

Richard and Judy loved it.

"That was amazing," said Judy. "Would

134

you like to come on the show and sing it for us here?"

"Yes, please," I said live on air.

"Could you do it next Monday?" she asked.

Today was Friday.

"Of course."

The following Sunday night, Mum, Auntie Caroline, and I took the train up to London. Mum took the Monday off work.

We had to be at the studio very early the next morning.

We had never been in a TV studio before, and I remember being amazed by how many people were in the studio and wondering what they all did.

The *Richard and Judy* TV set looks a bit like a lounge, with couches and windows with curtains and potted plants.

I think I was more excited than nervous, though it's sometimes difficult to tell which feeling's which. Well, it was when I was younger.

I was wearing a turquoise floor-length satin dress made by a friend of Mum's called Rose and a turquoise Alice band in my hair to match. When it was time for me to sing, I stood in the middle of the studio floor and sang "Somewhere" from *West Side Story*.

Afterward I went and sat on the sofa next

to Richard and Judy. This is where all the guests sit.

"Now, first of all, what a beautiful dress," said Judy. "You look like a princess."

"Thank you."

"And tell us how long you've been singing for?"

"Ever since I was three," I told her.

"And you come from a musical family, don't you? Tell us about the other singers in your family."

"Well, my granddad used to be in a rock 'n' roll band, and my auntie Caroline's a fabulous cabaret singer."

"And you're having singing lessons, is that right?"

"Yes. I have a singing teacher called Lulu who I go to once a week."

"And you're so confident. I think we're just going to have to take you home with us," said Judy.

When we got back to Cardiff, Dad told us that he had sneaked out of his office to watch the show and said that he was "amazed and proud."

"I had a lump in my throat seeing you," he said.

So had the producer of a kids' TV show called *Bright Sparks*. A few weeks after going on *Richard and Judy*, I was invited on *Bright*

Sparks to sing "Pie Jesu" and talk about my singing.

By now I was getting used to the types of questions I was asked by interviewers. Little did I know *how* often I'd soon be answering these very same questions again and again.

But I still enjoy it — most of the time.

And now back to Auntie Caroline.

You see, I wasn't the only one in the family having my first taste of going on TV. Auntie Caroline was getting ready to do the same thing herself.

What happened was that Auntie Caroline had entered herself as a contestant on the prime-time Saturday night TV show *The Big, Big Talent Show*. Different acts compete, and the winner is decided by the audience. But unlike regular talent shows, where each act is introduced by the TV host, on *The Big, Big Talent Show* a friend or relative introduces each act.

Which is why a researcher from *The Big, Big Talent Show* came to our house in Cardiff to meet me. Auntie Caroline had suggested that I come on the show and introduce her.

When the researcher — his name was Jake — came round to the house, we showed him the *Richard and Judy* tape. He loved it. He suggested that I sing a few lines of "Pie Jesu" before Auntie Caroline sang her song.

We thought it was a great idea.

July 17, 1997. Back to London.

The big day arrived, and Auntie Caroline was so nervous, she couldn't speak. She went very pale, she couldn't eat, and she was shaking like a leaf. The four of us traveled up by train, Mum, Dad, Auntie Caroline, and me. We arrived at Paddington Station, London, and took a taxi to the TV studio in West London.

The host of *The Big, Big Talent Show* is Jonathan Ross, and he's a lovely man. He's in his thirties, he wears very bright suits and ties that suit his over-the-top personality, and he has a bit of a lisp. I'm trying to think of an American TV host to compare him with. I suppose he's like a mixture of David Letterman and an MTV presenter, courteous and cheeky at the same time, if you know what I mean.

I wasn't wearing anything special that day.

I was dressed casually in a beige skirt and brown T-shirt, and I had my hair in a pony-tail.

First we rehearsed. Then came time to record the show. I was sitting in a chair opposite Jonathan Ross, and I was so small that my feet didn't touch the floor. The conversation went something like this:

"What kind of music does your auntie

sing?" asked Jonathan.

"She sings Spice Girls, she sings rock, she sings love songs," I said, and you should have heard my voice.

I had started at the Cathedral School, and you can tell by my accent. It had completely changed. You wouldn't have known I came from Wales. I sounded so posh, you'd have thought I was related to the Queen.

"And I hear you have a terrific voice, too, don't you?" said Jonathan. "But it's a different sort of style to your auntie's, isn't it?"

"Oh yes, very different. I'm a soprano. I'm into opera."

"So you're eleven years old and you're into opera."

"Yes."

"Will you give us a little burst?"

"Yes, of course. As soon as I get a C off the orchestra."

Then I stood up and sang four lines of "Pie Jesu," and I remember the audience clapping as I sat down.

"Wow, that's fantastic," said Jonathan. "Are you sure you haven't got someone else out there singing it for you?"

Since then I've been asked this question so many times. So, back to Jonathan.

"To follow that is going to be very difficult. Is your auntie as good as you?"

"She's better," I said. "She's fantastic, she's brilliant, she's a star in the making."

And then out came Auntie Caroline. She looked fabulous. She looked like a rock 'n' roll star.

She was wearing a pair of black leather pants, a black see-through blouse, and a black bra. She opened her arms and threw back her head and started singing "Roberta," an original love song written by John David.

After she had finished her song Jonathan said to her, "What a fantastic song. It deserves to get in the charts. Does the rest of the family sing?"

"Yes," said Auntie Caroline.

"You must be terrible to have as neighbors," he joked.

"Well, we have great parties," said Auntie Caroline.

Jonathan laughed.

Now, like I said, the winner of *The Big, Big Talent Show* contest is decided by the audience. Before the audience made their minds up, a newspaper show-biz columnist called Gary Bushell gave his opinion.

"Terrific," he said. "Caroline has a very strong voice. In fact, she's probably the strongest female vocalist we've had on this series so far."

It was actually the sixth week of the contest, so it was a really nice thing for him to say.

"It's a great song," he said. "And Caroline's got such great command that you'd have no doubts at all about her ability to perform live."

In the end, though, it was up to the audience.

Auntie Caroline came in second.

She was beaten by a comedienne called Jenny Jones. We thought it was very unfair, but as Auntie Caroline said, "You can't win them all."

We felt bad for her, especially me, because *The Big, Big Talent Show* was supposed to be Auntie Caroline's big break.

"They put you on before me," says Auntie Caroline when we talk about it now. "I was singing my guts out, and they were still talking about you. Am I bitter because you stole my limelight and my big break?

"No, it's fab."

I told you Auntie Caroline has a wicked sense of humor.

Still, what happened next, no one could have predicted. I mean, who would have guessed that *The Big, Big Talent Show* contest would turn out to be my big break?

14

Starting Out

I know I've been very lucky with my singing taking off the way it did after I was on *The Big, Big Talent Show*.

But I've also had to deal with the downside of success.

Fame can make life easier, but it can also make life harder. What I mean is that I've had to deal with some things that have been very unpleasant and hurtful to me and my family. Things a normal fifteen-year-old girl wouldn't have to cope with. This year my parents and I have been involved in a lawsuit with my ex-manager. The story has been written about in the newspapers and gossip magazines, and it has been a very stressful and hurtful time for all of us at home. We've had to deal with a lot of accusations made against my family, particularly my mother, all of which have been untrue.

Still, by supporting each other, we've kept each other strong.

It's difficult to know where to begin, and what to say, about my ex-manager of twenty-two months. First of all, when you start out doing something new, everything is new. Second, the less said about him the better, because he belongs to the past and so much good stuff has happened since that we try not to think about him at all.

All I will say is that the lawsuit was painful for all of us, but we made the right decision and it was my decision, not anyone else's, to sack my ex-manager. Since then everything has been so much better. My career has gone from strength to strength, especially this year. And I love working with my new management team, which consists of the head of Sony, Paul Burger; Mum and Dad; my lawyer, Mark Melton; and Terry Kenny.

Terry's taken over as my main adviser along with others. And you haven't met Terry's assistant, Josh Cole, who drives a convertible, records everything on his Sony digital camera, and even lets me decide what CDs we listen to on his car stereo. Josh is a mate.

It's like we're one big happy family now.

Everything is easier and we're so much

closer and the reason we're so close is that everyone trusts each other. Without trust everything falls apart. Still, this experience has taught me a valuable lesson, which is that the world isn't always a nice place. When you have problems, you have to be brave and strong and stand your ground.

Anyway, to get back to the story, the first thing we needed was a demo tape to send to the record companies. I ended up recording it in a studio in Cardiff. Lulu was there to help me vocally, and Auntie Caroline was there to help me emotionally. I was in an environment I knew, and I had my family there. This helped my singing. We recorded "Pie Jesu," "Somewhere Over the Rainbow," and John Lennon's "Imagine."

Then Mum paid for me to have some photos done.

Finally, when the demos and the photos were ready, we sent them out with tapes of my TV appearances to EMI, Sony, Decca, Polygram, and Warner in London.

By now, it was just after Christmas. We knew we wouldn't hear anything for a while.

In the meantime — another first for me.

October 4, 1997. My first big concert.

I was booked to sing at the Festival of Welsh Mixed Voices at the Royal Albert Hall, which is one of London's most famous venues. The musical director was John Peleg, and he telephoned Mom after seeing me on *Richard and Judy*. We thought he was joking, but he wasn't. He was serious. He wanted me to come and sing a solo along with 850 choirs from all over Wales.

I wore a white ball gown, and Mom says I looked like an angel. I had on a tiara, and my hair was curled. I sang "Pie Jesu," and "Somewhere" from *West Side Story*. It was my first experience of singing at a large concert, and I was only eleven years old.

A few weeks later I sang at the London Palladium, which is another fabulous venue. One day I was just a schoolgirl, and the next day I was a performer at one of the most palatial theaters in London. It was amazing.

It was a charity concert for the Anthony Nolan Bone Marrow Trust, and I was booked by Jan Kennedy, who was my agent for a time and has since become my friend. I sang "Ave Maria" and "Pie Jesu," and I wore a turquoise sequined dress that sparkled underneath the lights.

I'm trying to remember what it felt like to be eleven years of age and to sing for the first time in these two legendary places.

I remember feeling overwhelmed by the size of the stages and being dazzled by the bright lights. It was the first time that I'd been on stages that big and looked out into blackness like looking into outer space.

It was my first experience of the strange feeling of absence I get when I'm performing on stage. What I mean is, I'm there, but I'm not there. I don't feel numb exactly, but I don't feel anything or see anything or think anything.

It's like having an out-of-body experience, although I can't see myself on stage.

I remember Mum being very nervous. She was still smoking then, and when she was nervous she smoked a lot of cigarettes. She's given up since then, thank goodness.

After both concerts Mum said, "You looked like a little china doll. You looked perfect, and you stood so still and sang so beautifully. I felt so proud."

The next thing I remember was feeling so tired that all I wanted to do was go to bed. This was my first experience of the gigantic drop in adrenaline you get after you've been on stage. The best way to describe it is that it's like a massive sugar low after a massive sugar high.

I get a bit moody, and I just want to go home and be me again.

When people ask me what it's like to sing on stage, I tell them that it's a bit like sharing yourself with all the people in the audience. Afterward you feel drained, as if your soul has been squeezed, although in a great way.

15

Sony

The next part of my story is one of my favorite parts.

It's one of Mum's favorites, too.

I've been with Sony Music since 1998. I work with Sony people in the United Kingdom and Sony people in America, and they're like extra family.

They treat me and all my family so well.

As Mum always says, "A lot of your success has to do with your team. They're the best."

I totally agree.

We had a few other meetings before Sony, including one with EMI. But just after Christmas 1998, Paul Burger, the president of Sony Europe, received one of my demo tapes and called right away to say he wanted to meet me.

Paul says, "The tape I got surprised me

because of your age and talent. So whatever misgivings I might have had about a twelve-year-old, I thought, Let's just see."

February 4, 1998. Back to London. It was time to meet Paul.

The Sony offices are in the middle of Soho on Great Marlborough Street. The street is always jammed with black taxis and messengers on bikes and film people and music people. Everyone's in a rush.

Inside the Sony building, it's *really* calm. The elevators are mirrored and the walls look like shiny marble, and there's always music in the background and music videos playing on the big TV screens.

I remember feeling so excited.

I was wearing a brown suit and cream tights, and I'd spilled coffee on my tights and left a big stain. Mum was nervous; I could tell. She tries to hide her feelings, but I can tell from the look on her face and the tone of her voice. She narrows her eyes, and her voice gets tight.

We took the elevator upstairs and were shown into Paul's office.

Paul said hi and shook our hands and seemed friendly.

What were my first impressions?

I thought his office was amazing. Everything is blue — blue carpet, blue couch, blue chairs — and there's an enormous window, and the room is filled with sunlight. I thought he was a really nice man. He has a warm face. He is very tall, with curly black hair and, as Dad says, a very firm handshake. He's the sort of man who, you just know, knows what he wants. He's very confident — and he makes you feel confident.

We chatted for a while. He asked me the usual questions about my singing. Where did it come from? When did I start singing? What did I sing?

Then I got up and sang "Pie Jesu." He looked a bit surprised.

We've laughed about it since.

You see, later Paul told us that he wouldn't have asked me to sing if I hadn't offered.

Paul explains it like this.

"I was really impressed. I'd already found you charming and vivacious. Then when the meeting was over, you said, "Don't you want me to sing?" I thought it was going to be embarrassing, but you stood there five feet away from me, opened your mouth, and just exuded this angelic yet subtle voice. It completely blew my socks off. You were a clever girl. You had me hook, line, and sinker."

Well, I must have done something right, because we heard back from Paul within twenty-four hours. Sony wanted to sign me.

We screamed with excitement.

Well, Mum did, anyway.

"I was at work when the call came," she says. "And I screamed the place down. None of the girls in the office knew what the hell was going on until I explained who had just called. We thought we were going to have wait at least two weeks, and then the call came the next day that Sony wanted to sign her. It was unbelievable.

"I couldn't wait to get home and tell Charlotte."

Two weeks later we were back in the Sony offices in London for a meeting with Paul and the head of Sony Classical in America, Peter Gelb.

Sony offered me a five-album deal.

To make five albums, even I knew, was going to take more than a few years. Anything could happen during those years. And I must have realized this, because at this meeting I had a question for Paul.

"What happens if I get to fifteen and I don't want to work with you, or I start doing what you don't want, or I color my hair and act in a way that isn't sweet and lovely?" I asked.

Paul laughed. "Well, we'll just have to turn you into Alanis Morissette," he said.

I liked this answer, because I thought Alanis Morissette was cool.

But we still hadn't said yes to Sony.

It was at our *third* meeting that Sony really sold itself to us.

This time we were in the big conference room. Paul was there and Joanna Burns, the head of press, and Chris Black, who is the head of Sony Classical in the United Kingdom, and other Sony people.

On the wall in the conference room are photographs of big-name Sony artists: Barbra Streisand, Celine Dion (whom Paul signed), Jamiroquai (whom Paul signed), and Michael Jackson.

What Paul had done was take a photograph of me from a kids' TV show I'd been on called *Talking Telephone Numbers* — and had it blown up. In with the photographs of all the *really* famous singers was a photograph of me.

"Look, Mum," I said. I was thrilled.

We thought it was brilliant.

And that's when I signed with Sony.

Now there's something else I need to say here about my relationship with Mum and how it played a part with Sony right from the start. What we later found out from Paul was that he'd noticed the way Mum and I get along.

I'll let Mum explain.

"When Paul came down to Cardiff for the first time — when we were recording the first album — he confided in me and said, 'Do you realize that it was because of yours and Charlotte's attitude toward each other that I let the meeting go on as long as it did?'

"He said, 'I liked your attitude. If you'd come across as a pushy mother, I would have shown you the door in ten minutes. What I liked was that you sat back and let Charlotte speak.'"

And this is where our relationship with Paul — and with Sony — started.

As Mum says, "Paul just took over right from the start. The way Sony has marketed you was as his brainchild. It was Paul who said, 'We've got to keep you young and funky.' He immediately realized that what was going to sell was your sparkling personality."

I think Mum's teasing me a bit now.

As for my relationship with Paul, I suppose if I had to describe it, I'd say it was father-daughterlyish or like he's my uncle and I'm his niece. What I mean is — yes, he's the president of Sony Music and I'm a recording artist, but I've become really good friends with him, his wife, Ossi, his son, Ben, and especially his daughter, Noa, who is the same age as me.

That reminds me, I've got a note from Noa in my bag. Hang on, I'll get it out and read it to you.

C, how is everything going? My house is so quiet without you (I was over at her house recently) *and so much less smelly. Anyway I'm sending you this picture of us with Ricky Martin* (we all went to his concert). *He looks so fine. On Saturday night we went out. . . .*

Oh dear, I better not read the rest. Noa got into serious trouble for staying out late. I love Noa because she's such good fun.

I suppose what I'm trying to say is, Paul isn't just a Sony guy anymore. He's a good guy and a really good friend.

When we're in America, we always travel with another lovely man called John Vernile, who is vice president of promotions with Sony Music in New York. John has a huge smile that lights up the room, and even if I'm feeling tired and don't want to do any more press or talk to any more interviewers, John can always get me motivated.

Sometimes he gives me a piggyback ride. I might be fifteen, but with John it doesn't matter.

John is the other reason I feel so lucky to be with Sony. He's part of the family, too.

The other Sony person I want to mention

is Howard Stringer, who is chairman and CEO of Sony America. When we went to meet him in his office in New York, we couldn't believe it when he said that he was Welsh — and he was born in St. David's Hospital in Cardiff, like Mum and Dad and me.

How about that for a small world?

Here's my family: Nan, Dad, Mum, Uncle Mark with little Elliot, Auntie Caroline, Bampy, and me. © *MDP (London) Mike Daines Pix*

My parents' wedding day. I was a bridesmaid. Doesn't my mum look pretty? *Neil Stapleton Photography*

When I was three, with Bampy at Nan and Bampy's house on Christmas Day. Mum and Dad had brought me a microphone to play with.

My first bike at three years old on Christmas Day at Nan and Bampy's house.

I loved Father Christmas when I was five (still do).

Me and Mum dressed up for the Lord Mayor's Parade in Cardiff when I was six.

My official school photograph from St. Mary's Roman Catholic Primary School (I was six).

Me and Mum in Spain in November 1994, age eight. The doll was given to me by a group of golfers from Cardiff because I sang for them.

Me and one of my best friends, Kim, when I was fourteen. *David Hollins/Wales News Service*

Mum and Dad and me! © *2000 Waring Abbott*

Here I am with President Clinton and Mrs. Clinton in July 1999. I was so thrilled to be at the White House. *Sharon Farmer/White House*

When I was twelve, my first PBS special, *Voice of an Angel*, aired. *George Bodnar*

'NSync and me on the *Touched by an Angel* set in September 1999. They're so cute!

I recorded my third album, Dream a Dream, in
July 2000 at Abbey Road Studios. *John Vernile*

This is my special
advisor and friend
Terry Kenny, in
London in July
2000. *John Vernile*

I'm a lucky girl — here I am with Ricky Martin at his concert at Earl's Court in London, September 2000. *Photographer: Chris Lopez/used by permission of Sony Music*

I met the Pope when I was twelve (January 1999) at the Vatican. He stroked my face and called me "the little singer." © *L'osservatore Romano*

16

Back to School

I've been so busy telling you about my music and the launch of my career that I've skipped two really important chapters of my life — the two schools I've been to since leaving St. Mary's.

The funny thing is that considering my number of absences from school, 104 last year, you'd think I was someone who *didn't* like school.

I'm the opposite. I *enjoy* school.

What I mean is, I like the atmosphere. I like seeing my friends and hanging out at lunchtime and catching up on all the gossip. I even like some of the classes and some of the teachers.

When I can't go to school because I'm traveling, I have two private tutors, Richard Leyshon and Catherine Aubury. But you can read about them later on.

First of all, I want to tell you about Llandaff Cathedral School, and afterward I'll tell you about Howell's, which is where I go now.

I went to the Cathedral School for two years from the age of ten. It was Mum and Dad who decided I should go there, because they wanted the best for me. Cathedral School is a fee-paying school, and it has a very good reputation academically and musically. It has fantastic facilities. There are fifteen acres of parkland and sports fields. It has a huge music room and art studios and a swimming pool. And it has two choirs, a boys' choir and a girls' choir.

When Mum and Dad found out that there was a scholarship for singing, they put me forward for the audition, which I passed. The next step was finding the money to pay the fee, which is £1,400 a term.

I'll let Mum explain.

"This was obviously before you were signed to Sony and started making records, and at the time we couldn't afford the money needed for the fees. So the headmaster, Mr. Gray, kindly put your case to the board of governors, who were so impressed by your singing audition, they subsidized the cost.

"But we still needed another thousand

pounds. So what I did was write to every company and businessman I could in England and Wales and ask for sponsorship. In the end, we managed to get sponsorship from a kind local businessman called Stanley Thomas."

I told you Mum was a good businesswoman.

"We then met Terry at the end of your first year at the Cathedral School through a mutual friend. Terry runs a charity organization called the Rufford Foundation, which sponsors different causes, mainly conservation projects, and sometimes talented children. Unfortunately, Stanley Thomas said he couldn't contribute toward the fees for your second year at Cathedral School. I explained your situation to Terry, and he wrote a glowing letter to the board of trustees, and they went for it. It was thanks to Terry that your fees for the second year were paid — this time by the Rufford Foundation."

You'll read more about Terry further on.

I started at the Cathedral School in September 1996. It was very different from St. Mary's.

The school is in a very old building next to Llandaff Cathedral, and it looks a bit like a stately home. I had to wear a maroon blazer with the Cathedral School emblem on the pocket, a gray shirt, a gray skirt, and a maroon tie. I was in a class of eleven pupils, and I was one of only two girls. Cathedral School is still really a boys' school. Girls have only been allowed to go the Cathedral School for a few years.

We had to work very hard.

We had choir practice every morning for twenty minutes in the school chapel. The chapel is, as you can imagine, extremely beautiful, and I always enjoyed singing there. Once a week, on a Monday evening at six P.M., the girl's choir would sing evensong in the cathedral. We wore dark blue robes with white ruffs, and the public were free to come and listen to us. Sometimes there would be five people there, other times thirty.

It was never very busy.

The boys' choir sang evensong every other night, and their robes were red. I think more people came to listen to the boys.

We also studied Latin, and we had two hours of homework every night. Even so, when I think back to my time at Cathedral School, I think I was happy there. The girls had to work hard to keep up with the boys, but we had fun as well. And now that I'm at an all-girls school, I miss the boys, though I had some really good girlfriends at the Cathedral School. There was Susanna Gray, who was the headmaster's daughter. She had a beautiful voice, but she sang Handel arias while I sang Puccini. Then there was Helena Ryan whom Mr. Goss — the games teacher — called Helena-Queen-of-all-Chicks. He had names for everyone, although I've forgotten mine. And then there was Gemma Hawkins.

At break we used to sit together and chat. We were always together.

But now I'm getting nostalgic. I'm forgetting all the things I didn't like about the Cathedral School — like being called by your last name. The teachers called me Church.

If I put up my hand in class to answer a question, Mr. Lovell, the English teacher, who made us recite poems, would point at me and say, "Yes, Church?"

You see, in British boys' schools it's traditional for teachers to call pupils by their last names. In the beginning I found it strange, but I suppose I must have got used to it because I never think about it now.

My music teacher was Mr. Hoeg. Mum will never forget what he said to her.

"It was at a parents' evening," says Mum, "and I remember saying to him how much you liked your singing and that's what you wanted to do. Mr. Hoeg, who I know was only trying to let me down gently, said, 'You do realize that ninety-nine percent of people don't make it?'

"And I said, 'I believe that my daughter is part of that one percent.' He looked a little surprised, but there you go."

It was Mr. Gray, the headmaster, who took the girls' choir. By now I'd also started singing lessons with Lulu once a week, and I was developing my voice and my control. Mr. Gray said that my vibrato wasn't right for the choir and that I should sing straight like all the other girls.

As Mum says, "Lulu will never forgive Mr. Gray for trying to knock the vibrato out of your voice."

Mr. Gray wanted me to blend in with the rest of the choir. But I'm like Mum, not good at being told to blend in.

It makes me want to do the opposite. I remember then I didn't like being told not to sing with vibrato — particularly when Lulu was teaching me how to perfect my vibrato.

But I liked Mr. Gray. He was very good to me. He can still remember my audition. He was really encouraging.

Here he is.

"You were a very musical little girl, but it wasn't just the voice that impressed us, it was the whole personality. Then we discovered that you had three voices. The one you normally hear, with a certain amount of vibrato. Then a very straight voice that was ideal for blending in with the choir. And the third, a heavy chest voice that you would use for songs from American musicals."

Yes — the musicals.

I think what I actually loved the most about my time at the Cathedral School were the musicals. They were some of the best fun I've ever had on stage. We did a production of *Oklahoma!* and a production of *Bugsy Malone*, and they were big productions with great costumes, fabulous sets, and lots of rehearsing.

Everyone says my American accent is pretty good, and I love doing it. Even now my friends tease me because when I say "beautiful" I say it with an American accent. I say "bee-u-di-ful." I guess I've been spending so much time over there that it's starting to rub off.

Anyway in *Oklahoma!* I played Ado Annie, the flirt who can't say no. She's a dizzy dame, and so, so funny.

In *Bugsy Malone* I played Blousey, and I wore a curly red wig and a red flapper's hat and a pink dress. I had to say things like "You promised me, Bugsy, you promised me."

All the boys were in trilbies and pinstripe suits just like in the movie. You even heard the sounds of gunshots when guns were fired on stage.

I told you the Cathedral School did everything really well.

In the end, the reason I had to leave the Cathedral School was that it didn't go up to the age of sixteen. You had to leave when you were thirteen. It's changed now and you can stay until you're sixteen; if I were still there, I might have stayed on just because academically it's so good.

I said good-bye to the Cathedral School in the summer of 1998, and I felt sad but happy at the same time. By this time my music career had started. I was about to record my first album, and there was no way I could do choir practice *and* two hours of homework every night — and find time to rehearse with Lulu.

Still, what I left with were lots of happy memories, lots of fantastic singing experience, and a very good head start in my education. When I got to Howell's — my next school — I was so far ahead in French and history and other classes that I couldn't believe it.

And it's because of this that my trust fund is paying for my nephew Elliot to go to the Cathedral School. I want the best for him — just like Mum and Dad got the best for me.

17

Howell's

My next school was Howell's.

Mum likes Howell's because Howell's has "a 100 percent pass rate" in examinations. I like Howell's because all my friends go there.

I started at Howell's in September 1998 when I was twelve.

It's an old school, although not as old as the Cathedral School, which is hundreds of years old. Howell's has been around since 1860. It's a gray stone building sitting on eighteen acres of grounds, and it has a clock tower above the entrance.

Have you ever seen that black-and-white English film *The Belles of St. Trinian's*? Well, if you have, you'll have an idea of the sort of school I'm talking about, although we don't wear straw hats and I hate field hockey.

I've only been at Howell's for a couple of years, but all my closest friends are from

Howell's. My three best friends are Abby, Jo, and Kim, whom you can meet properly later on when I take you into town with us on a Saturday.

Howell's has six hundred girls. No boys.

When I started at Howell's, I had to get used to being at an all-girls school. When girls tease each other it can be cruel, but when boys take the mickey, it's jokey. Boys take things lightly. Girls take everything much more seriously.

But I really like Howell's.

The headmistress is Mrs. Fitz, and she's been pretty understanding about my career and the media interest in me. It's a good thing she has a good sense of humor.

Since I've been at Howell's, there have been some really funny practical jokes. Well, they seemed funny at the time, probably because I was younger.

Once, the whisper went round — I don't know who started it — that everyone should bring an alarm clock to school. The next morning in assembly all six hundred of us set off our alarm clocks at once. Everybody started laughing, including Mrs. Fitz.

Another time some of the girls drew a huge picture of one of the teachers wearing a bikini and smoking a cigarette, and they hung it up in the dinner hall before lunch.

Mum says Auntie Caroline used to dream of going to Howell's, but Nan and Bampy couldn't afford it. Only the posh girls went to Howell's. I wish Auntie Caroline could have gone there. I try never to forget how lucky I am, but it's not been exactly easy.

Only three months after I'd started at Howell's, my first album, *Voice of an Angel*, came out. I became the youngest solo artist to go straight in at number one in the classical charts, and two weeks later my album went to number four in the pop charts.

And let's just say that the press went a bit crazy.

The new chart countdown is *always* announced on a Sunday. On the Monday after the Sunday when I'd reached number four in the pop charts, Sony warned us that there might be a film crew — or maybe a couple of photographers — at the school gates.

On Monday morning Mum drove me to school like she always did. We got to the school gates, and there waiting for me were eight, maybe nine, film crews in white trucks with satellite dishes on the roofs and loads of photographers.

It was a circus. I couldn't believe it; neither could Mum. Mum had to come into school and help out.

I'll let her tell you about it.

"The deputy headmistress, Mrs. Davis; the headmistress, Mrs. Fitz; and I ended up having to escort the film crews into your math class so that they could film you looking like a regular schoolgirl having a regular day at school."

Each crew came in for five minutes.

Click, click, click.

We carried on with our lesson, then the next one.

Click, click, click.

The next day a film crew from one of the breakfast TV shows came to school and filmed me singing with my class in the assembly hall. Then they interviewed me and some of my friends and asked me how I felt.

"It's really exciting," was all I could say. It was all such a rush.

All the girls in my class thought it was kind of cool having class interrupted and being on TV, although I don't think my math teacher has ever forgiven me. She had a very long face. She definitely did not seem happy about having her class disturbed, not that she's mentioned it since.

Later on, a few of the girls said that my success had gone to my head. One of the rumors was that I'd pushed in front of someone in line in the lunch canteen and said, "Excuse me, don't you know who I am?" But I guess I've got to expect that kind of thing.

I mean, a lot of the younger girls come up and want to talk to me about where I've been and who I've met when I'm in the library trying to do my homework. Someone will come up and say, "Can I have your autograph?"

But I've had to get used to that sort of stuff, too. Sometimes I wonder what it means.

I can't describe it because it's impossible to describe. I feel normal. My friends don't pay much attention to it. I just get on with life. I don't think about what I do — and how people perceive me — I just do it.

But I'm aware of other stuff going on. I know when I'm psyching people out and they feel strange around me.

When there are stories in the newspapers about me, I sometimes overhear the girls at school whispering nasty things about me. It gets me really upset.

People say don't worry about what you read in the newspapers because today's newspapers are tomorrow's chip papers (at the fish-and-chip shops, the fish and chips are wrapped in newspaper). But when it's about you, it makes you feel sick. It's awful.

It was actually Geri Halliwell — you

know, Ginger Spice — who gave me some really good advice. She said *never* read stories about yourself in the newspapers. If they're good stories, they will go to your head and give you a big ego. If they're horrible, they will upset you.

She was right.

Which is why I always like going to Howell's. At school, I can be as normal as Abby or Jo or Kim — or Gemma or Naomi or Emily. They're all fab. I love them all. They're great.

Now what can I tell you about my lessons? I can't do Latin anymore because I'm too busy — Latin is like an extra subject — and in my spare lessons Lulu comes up to the school and gives me singing lessons in the music room.

The French teacher always uses French conversation lessons to ask me about where I've been.

"Tu es fatigué?" she says, probably because she's just caught me yawning.

"Oui."

"Pourquoi?"

"Parce que je suis allée aux États-Unis."

"Et qu'est-ce que tu as fait là?"

"J'ai chanté à la Hollywood Bowl."

"Ah! Toutes mes félicitations."

"Merci, madame."

"Mais maintenant il faut que tu t'appliquér à faire la classe."

"Oui, madame."

You get the idea.

I like geography because I love Mrs. Davis, my geography teacher. She makes the subject come alive. It's also because I've been to so many different countries and have seen so many different places for myself that it all makes sense. Also Richard, my tutor, has a degree in geography. It's his favorite subject, and he has facts at his fingertips about everywhere we go.

For example: Jerusalem is 780 meters above sea level and is built on top of a limestone ridge and has dry heat because it's positioned between the Mediterranean and the desert.

Then, like I said earlier, I love ancient history. Can you imagine what it must have been like to live in Roman times and see gladiators fight? And the women used to put belladonna in their eyes to make their eyes bigger and brighter — and belladonna is deadly nightshade, which is a poison. They didn't have mascara in Roman times.

In English I write poems, but never sad ones. I'm good at moral stories. Last term we had to write a story about a hunchback in the park. We had to write the story from either the hunchback's point of view or the bully's view. I wrote from the hunchback's point of view. I think most of my friends did.

Then we had to write a diary, and I wrote the diary of Juliet while she was waiting for Romeo, with all the thoughts that were going through her head. She loved Romeo so much that she wanted to die. And she was only my age.

Mum wants me to read the interesting parts of my year-end report card here. I can't; Mum will have to read it herself.

Religious Studies: A1. Charlotte has had some good ideas and is able to understand religious concepts . . .

"And this was before she went to Jerusalem."

. . . and likes to contribute to discussion in class.

"True. She loves talking."

History: A1. Charlotte has participated intelligently and perceptively and has clearly gained a clear understanding of the topics studied. Her examination result indicates a thorough factual knowledge. . . .

Fitness: Charlotte is a competent performer in dance and has produced excellent work in the group and demonstrated the ability to plan and perform. She has worked hard to develop her skills in tennis. . . .

Okay, Mum, I'll make the comments. The only sports I like are swimming and squash.

Music: A1. Charlotte is a delightful pupil, keen, conscientious, very talented and always gives her best, contributes well in class. Despite her absences from school I am delighted she has done so well in her written exam.

Last one.

Geography: A1. Charlotte is an able pupil and an enthusiastic geographer. She contributes fully to class discussion, and I have been impressed by the high standard of her written work.

My geography teacher, Mrs. Davis, is my favorite teacher.

English: A1. Charlotte has worked with enthusiasm and takes a lively interest in the texts we have read this year. She has produced very pleasing work. Class contributions most welcome and display a maturity and insight beyond her years.

Math: B1.

Oops.

Oh well, I managed to get A1s in most of my subjects. Mum was pleased, and I told you my tutors are fab.

18

My Tutors, Richard and Catherine

You know how difficult it is trying to decide who to go on holiday with. I mean, you have to make sure that whoever you take isn't going to get on your nerves and bore you to tears — or want to do completely different things from you.

Well, it's a bit like that choosing a private tutor — multiplied by ten.

What I mean is, my private tutors, Richard and Catherine, are two people I spend a lot of time with. I study with them, travel with them, eat with them, play squash with Richard, and we have a laugh together.

I'm going to introduce you to Richard first because he's been my tutor since January 1999. Somehow — and I do wonder how sometimes — we get along just fine.

We were lucky to find Richard. It was Mum who found him. Here she is to tell the story.

"It was when I was still working for Cardiff City Council [local government]," she says. "Richard had just finished his teaching diploma in geography and couldn't find a teaching job because he was just starting out, so he came to work for the housing department. He was put at a desk next to mine.

"Well, we got talking, like you do, and he told me that he was a fully qualified, trained teacher. At that time Charlotte was studying for her entrance exams to get into Howell's. There were a couple of girls going for the one place, and we wanted to make sure Charlotte got it. She had a problem with math and needed a bit of extra coaching. So I said to Richard, 'Would you like to come round and do a bit of tuition with her?' and he said, 'Fine.' "

The following week Richard came round to the house.

He says he remembers me as "a lively girl with tremendous enthusiasm."

Hmmm.

When I first met him I thought he was very neat and serious, with a good sense of humor. And he is.

He's in his mid-twenties. He's not that much taller than me and always smartly dressed in a casual way. He wears button-down shirts and jeans that are never scruffy, and he takes a while to get to know you, but when you know him, he's really funny. He loves comedy. He's always lending me tapes of the comedian Eddie Izzard or the BBC news quiz *Have I Got News for You?* or the Austin Powers films. We both like silly humor with clever wordplay. We hit it off straightaway.

He helped me with my math, and I passed my entrance exam and got into Howell's.

Mum says that what she said to Richard next, she said as a joke. What she said was, "When Charlotte becomes famous, she can have you as a tutor."

She didn't think for a minute that I would become famous or that Richard would become my private tutor, and neither did I. But then my first album came out, and my life went a bit crazy.

And now Richard is my private tutor for math and science and geography. Catherine teaches me English, history, and French.

Catherine is really cool.

She's cool in that skinny, blond kind of way. She's only five feet one, and she's very delicate and pretty. She wears pencil skirts and high heels to make her look older. Not that it works. She's twenty-four years old but looks about seventeen. When we're studying together on planes, the stewardesses ask, "Are you studying together?" because they think we're best friends. They don't imagine for one minute that she's my tutor.

In America, when she tries to buy a drink in a bar, she has to show her ID. I tell her she should be flattered. She thinks it's an insult.

"I don't want to look like a kid," she says.

She went to college with Richard, which is how we met her. And — like Richard — she's got a great sense of humor. When she's traveling with me and Mum and not Dad, she'll even stay in the same room as us. She comes from a family that's really close, like mine. She understands the importance of family, which is why Mum thinks, and I agree, she's fitted in with us so well.

Catherine has been teaching me for less than a year. English is her favorite subject. It's my second favorite subject after history. She's always recommending great books for me to read. We've just started reading Emily Brontë's *Wuthering Heights*. It's one of my set texts for my English GCSE. I didn't think I'd like it, but it's so romantic. I can't put it down.

Like I said earlier, in Britain when we're sixteen we do exams called GCSEs to get into high school. Richard and Catherine have started preparing me for these. And anyway, by law, I have to do three hours of schoolwork a day, or fifteen hours a week. So wherever we are in the world, whether it's Jerusalem or Los Angeles or Rio, we get my books together, sit down at the desk in my hotel room — and study. It's a funny way to do my lessons, but I've got used to it now . . . ish.

Is it difficult to concentrate? Yes.

I mean, sometimes I think I have a low boredom threshold because I'm interested in so many things. But the good thing is that when I need to concentrate, I can. I can switch my concentration from one thing to the next pretty easily.

As Richard and Catherine both know, going from being on stage at the Hollywood Bowl, where I was singing in front of eighteen thousand people, to studying math in my villa at the Sunset Marquis Hotel is not easy. Especially when I can hear the voices of people splashing in the pool and I can see the sun shining and I know that Robbie Williams is lying in the Jacuzzi because I've just had a chat with him and he gave a note to my mum:

Your voice is amazing. Please do not start smoking. When you hear my live vocals, you'll know I'm not joking.

I want to be out there with Robbie, not in here with my books.

Still, if Richard or Catherine see my attention wandering, they'll turn to something else or we'll break for five minutes. As soon as I switch off, they know that whatever they do is a waste of time because nothing's getting through.

What also happens when we've been traveling for a long time is that my concentration goes out the window. I get silly.

We all get silly — Mum, Dad, Richard, Catherine, and me. We call it jet-lag humor, because we're all on different time zones and none of us can talk any sense.

I was telling someone last week about plans for the fall, and I said I would be back in America around "late September, early orchestra." What I meant to say was "late September, early October."

I used to play jokes on Richard all the time when I was younger, but I'm less of a practical joker now. But there was one time when we caught him out so badly, I have to tell you about it. Richard fell for it *completely*.

We were in America and we asked an American friend of ours to call up and pretend that he was from the U.S. Education Board.

"Hello, I'm from the Education Department in Washington, D.C. We hear you're

186

tutoring Miss Charlotte Church, is that correct?" said our friend.

"Er . . . yes," said Richard.

"I have to ask you, sir, can you tell us where you went to university?"

"I went to Swansea University in Wales."

"I'm sorry, sir, but we don't know that university. We cannot allow you to tutor Miss Charlotte Church unless you have the confirmed credentials."

"Er . . . well . . . I've got some papers here," said Richard.

Poor Richard. We're so cruel.

Though when it's time to study, my tutors can be pretty cruel, too. They have to be. Their job is to get me through my exams and make sure I'm not behind in my lessons back home. Even if I've been up since six A.M. doing radio interviews and photo shoots, I have to find the concentration to focus on my studies.

The day I met President Clinton in June 1999, I had to sit for my end-of-year math and geography and French exams from Howell's in the morning. The exam papers were flown out to Washington in a sealed envelope, and Richard was my invigilator. He had to oversee me sit the exam in room 603 at the InterContinental Hotel in Washington, D.C.

The exams were ninety minutes each. I wanted a bit more time for math — my least favorite subject.

"Please," I begged him.

"Sorry, Charlotte. That's it," he said.

And there was nothing I could do about it.

Normally — on a day-to-day basis — when we do our three hours together, we'll cover two or three subjects. We sit side by side at the desk. Catherine will say, "Okay, let's do a French exercise. Irregular verbs. Here you are."

Then, while I do the exercise, she'll prepare something else. Then I'll give her what I've done, she will mark it, and I'll do the next exercise.

If I've made any mistakes, she will say, "Go and stand in the corner!"

It's our little joke, and we still find it funny. There we are in some hotel room with a TV in the corner and my rack of clothes hanging up and the maid knocking on the door asking if she can come in and clean, even though there is a "Do Not Disturb" sign on it — and I'm doing French past participles.

We couldn't be farther away from a class-room.

Like I said, it's our shared sense of humor that keeps us sane. Richard and Catherine are like family friends. If we've got an evening off, we'll hang out together. If we've got a day off, we'll go sight-seeing together — the way we recently did in Hong Kong.

As Mum says, "When we're away, it's like Richard and Catherine are living with us, which is a lot to ask of anyone. They do a brilliant job."

19

Remember Terry

Remember when Terry helped Mum find money for me to go to Llandaff Cathedral School?

Now Terry is my main adviser and chairman of my trust.

Mum says, "Every day I thank God for Terry. If we hadn't met Terry, we wouldn't be in this position now. He is the most wonderful, wonderful man I've ever met, and he can't do enough for you — or me."

As I think you've probably guessed, we love Terry. He's a big softie.

When we go to London, we stay in his flat.

When we first started going up to London from Cardiff, we would stay at hotels organized for us by Sony. It was never much fun. Then Terry offered to have us at his flat, and once we'd started staying with him, it felt like the most natural thing in the world.

It feels like home.

Now if we've got a plane to catch the next morning from Heathrow, we'll drive up from Cardiff the night before and stay with him. Or if we've just got off a long flight from somewhere and can't face driving back to Cardiff that night — it's a two-hour drive from Cardiff to Heathrow airport — we'll stay with him.

Terry's flat is in a tall building next to the river Thames. It has a view of the river and the London Eye — the gigantic Ferris wheel built to commemorate the millennium — and it isn't far from the Houses of Parliament. Sometimes we go Rollerblading by the river (well, I go Rollerblading and Terry walks). Other times we go CD shopping at Tower Records. He makes me tea and my favorite bacon sandwiches and lets me watch MTV and gives his opinion on the new clothes I've bought.

Terry is in his forties, with a boyish face. He calls me "Charl." He has lots of energy, and he likes to laugh. He wears shirts with top pockets, and he always has a pen in his pocket because he likes making notes. He's a top organizer.

He's one of those people you want to tell everything to. But I don't tell him everything. I think it's important to keep some things to myself. Everybody needs secrets. They're part of who you are.

What I mean is, Terry is like a father to me, and at the same time I tell him things I would never tell Dad. Stuff to do with friends and boys. I know it sounds weird, but Terry is like a half father, half girlfriend, sort of friend.

Sometimes if I'm in a bad mood, normally because I'm tired, Terry will say, "Remember, you're doing this because you've got a talent and you're giving other people so much pleasure. You have to live for the moment and enjoy *everything*."

And even though it sounds like common sense, Terry has this way of making more sense than anyone else. I guess it's because he's family, but he isn't. There's that little bit of distance, and that's good for me.

I'll tell you a bit more about why he's so wonderful.

Terry is the son of a coal miner, and he was brought up in the north of England. He started out working in a bank in a town called Nottingham. Later on he moved to Cardiff to work for the Stamford Chartered Bank. When we met him, he had just become head of the Rufford Foundation, which, as I explained, is a charitable foundation. It gives away £2 million each year.

We met Terry through a mutual friend, Luke Evans, who was also having singing lessons with Lulu. We invited Luke and Terry to *The Big, Big Talent Show*.

Mum says that she mentioned my situation to Terry then.

Terry remembers it this way.

"Maria was quite coy about it. She was slightly embarrassed, and all she said was, 'I hear you work for a charitable foundation. Well, I know it might sound like a real cheek, but Charlotte goes to the Cathedral School and we're finding it difficult to scrape together the fees to keep her there.'

"She explained to me that because of your voice, she wanted to send you to a music school. And she said that she had written to well over a hundred businessmen, asking for sponsorship — and hadn't had any luck."

When we met Terry at Lulu's house he had heard me sing. He says he couldn't believe how I went from being a normal, giggly little eleven-year-old to being so composed and singing with my *huge* voice.

"I stopped talking midsentence," he says. "I just couldn't believe the voice that was coming from that small body. In those days you were tiny. Your voice quite literally gave me goose bumps, and everything that had been explained to me about your voice I heard for myself.

"When Maria asked me if there was any chance that the foundation would consider helping you, I immediately said yes. What I needed Maria to do, though, was to write a letter for me to present to the trustees with details of the Cathedral School fees and her and James's incomes. I said that I would see what I could do.' "

Terry presented Mum's letter to the trustees with references from the school and a letter from Lulu, and — to Mum's relief and happiness — the trustees said yes. The Rufford Foundation would pay the outstanding £1,700 that was needed to complete a year's tuition.

What a lifesaver.

And that was just the beginning.

As soon as my first album came out — and went double platinum — and I started making some money, Mum and Dad had to decide what to do with the money and how to manage it.

Terry is so good with money, and he was already managing the Rufford Foundation and the trust funds of some of the foundation's trustees, he suggested managing mine as well.

Terry just says, "I suggested to Maria,

would it not make sense to set up a trust fund for you, and I explained the idea of it — that you wouldn't be able to touch the money until you were twenty-one — and Maria liked the idea. Obviously she didn't want the money to go straight into a bank account because you might start to spend it.

"The next thing that was agreed was that I'd make contact with a good lawyer who specializes in trust funds and a good stock-broker and a good accountant, and I became chairman of trustees."

March 1999. We had a little ceremony with Mark Melton and Terry and Mum. I had to sign some forms — and it all started from there. Terry has been organizing my money ever since. He gives me £60 a month from the trust as my allowance, and I spend it on clothes and CDs and makeup.

People always want to know how much I'm worth, and if you believed everything you read in the newspapers, you'd think I was worth £10 million one week and £20 million the next.

I'm worth nowhere near that.

Sometimes Terry sits me down and tells me what's going into my trust and what's going out. But to be honest, all I know is that the money in the trust is more than enough. When I turned fifteen my allowance increased, and that made me happy.

All I care about is having Terry in charge of the trust and being able to go to him when important things come up, like buying our dream house or paying for Elliot to go to the Cathedral School.

But Terry does more than organize my money now, he organizes me. Terry became one of my advisers after I sacked my ex-manager in January 1999.

Terry had been spending more and more time with us and traveling abroad with us anyway.

It was Mum who first suggested to Terry that he became more involved, and I know that at first he was a bit unsure. Still, that was over a year ago, and even though we don't know what's going to happen in the future, Terry's been brilliant.

And he's got Josh Cole. Josh works with Terry. Before that, he worked in TV and PR for ten years. Josh sorts out my day-to-day schedule.

I don't know how Terry puts up with me.

He gets to see me "warts and all," as he puts it. Then he'll say something really sweet, like "I'm still amazed every time I see you go on stage and stop being the Charlotte I know and become this star. Someone who just has this ability to capture the audience and make everyone who listens to you almost emotional. I've seen a number of people with tears when they listen to you when you've performed."

"Really?"

"Yes. Shall I tell them about Boston?"

"Oh, go on, then."

This is actually quite a funny story.

"In June we were in Boston. It was a charity event called Circle of Friends, and it was to raise funds for children's hospitals around America. I was with you and Maria, waiting in the dressing room for the limo to drive us down to the marquee where the stage was. We were in the house, and the marquee was in the garden.

"We eventually got the call saying the car was ready. We jumped in the car and started driving. After about three minutes, I said to Maria, 'Where are we going?'

"Maria said, 'I don't know. You better ask the driver.'

"So I said to the driver, 'Where are you going?'

"The driver said, 'I'm going to the hotel.'

"I said, 'Listen, we haven't performed yet!'

"I panicked. Maria panicked.

"You were totally calm.

"And the driver kept on driving because he couldn't turn anywhere because it was such a long stretch limo.

"Well, when we got to the marquee everyone was in a mad panic. You could see it on their faces. We'd kept the audience waiting about ten minutes. But you were still calm. You'd kept your composure completely. Then you went on stage to a major round of applause, you told the audience exactly what had happened, and you had them eating out of your hand. The audience thought it was hysterical."

The other thing Terry does is protect me from overwork.

"Yes, I spend a lot of time reminding people that you're a fourteen-year-old girl," he says. "I have to tell them that your schooling is a priority, that you want to do your GCSEs and go on and do A-Levels [high school diploma] and maybe go on to university. I'm always cutting schedules down.

"There are limitations on what you can do. You're not eighteen. You're not meant to start too early in the mornings, you've got to take breaks. You're allowed to work eighty days a year by law, and it's part of my role to make sure we don't exceed those days and that you do your three hours of schooling with Richard and Catherine every day — and ideally in the mornings, when your mind is most active. Schooling is a priority.

"Work and school is a balancing act, and we've established little rules, like if you're performing in America, you fly over one day, the next day is a *complete* rest day with maybe schooling only but no promotion work, and then the following day you perform, the following day you fly back.

"You could work every day, but you'd collapse — and why should you? You want normality, don't you?"

"Yes!"

Terry's part of the family now. He does everything.

As Mum says, "Terry helps with our finances." But it's more than that.

He stays with us at Christmas. He was with us in St. Lucia and Grenada last summer, and little Elliot adores him. He follows him everywhere, calling his name.

Which reminds me. I can hear him downstairs, talking to Mum. He's just driven here from London, and he's brought some of my clothes back from his flat.

"Terreeeeeeeeeeeeeeeeee, where's my pink T-shirt?"

"In a minute. Hang on. I've got it here."

Poor Terry. Like Mum said, we run him ragged, but it's only because we love him so much.

20

Album Time

After my first album went to number one in the classical charts and number four in the pop charts, I went into the *Guinness Book of Records* as the youngest artist to have a number one album in the classical charts.

As Mum says, "It was all a bit of a whirlwind. It was a lot to take in. In fact, it's only in the last six months that your success has properly started to sink in."

As it turned out, I had to take November and December 1998 off school to do all the interviews and photo shoots. I did interviews with the British newspapers like *The Times* and *The Sun* and magazines, and I went on British chat shows like *The Des O'Connor Show* — it's a bit like *The Tonight Show with Jay Leno.*

The first big music business event I went to was in November 1998, and it was called the Rainbow Ball. It was at the Dorchester Hotel in London, and I had my photograph taken with George Michael.

"Be happy," he said.

I was.

We had a great Christmas.

We had a big dinner at Nan and Bampy's house like we always do, with Auntie Caroline and Mark and Elliot and Mum and Dad, but as Mum says, "We were all so thrilled with your success that it made Christmas that extra bit special."

But before all that came the experience of recording my first album.

People always think it must have been a big deal because I hadn't done one before. At the time, the only thing that felt weird was singing not to an audience, but to a control booth instead.

Lulu remembers that "singing to nothing in particular was hard on you. You're a show girl who loves people, and everyone could see that from the way you performed. But you managed to focus like you always do and did a great job."

I've got a great team.

The Sony people I record my albums with make me feel so relaxed. Sian Edwards, my conductor, is Irish, with wild red hair and hands that she waves for me to follow.

My producer is Grace Row from New York and she has a voice I love because she's the one in the control booth facing me and talking me through the songs as I'm recording them. It's a soft voice with a firm edge, and she uses it, very skillfully, to get the best from me.

Grace is married to Charles Harbutt, who is also from New York, and he's the postproduction engineer.

Oh yes, and then there's Jeremy Caulton, who is my executive producer. He's English and looks like a professor with half-moon glasses and gray hair and a white suit. He speaks very properly and corrects me on my French and Italian pronunciation.

We've recorded three albums together. I couldn't do it without them. They are the reason that even though it's hard work, it's not hard work.

And then, of course, there's Lulu.

Lulu sits beside me in the recording studio with her cans of diet Coke and her suggestions and corrections and encouragement. I certainly couldn't do it without her.

We recorded my first album in five days in August 1998 during my summer holiday. I recorded it with the Welsh National Orchestra. What happened was that the orchestral arrangements were recorded first and I recorded my songs on top.

We decided to do the first album in a BBC recording studio in Cardiff, which was only five minutes from home, so that I wouldn't have to travel too far — and I'd feel relaxed.

Which is why I wore my bunny slippers.

One of the slippers was called Robbie, and the other one was called Bobby, and I wore them to make me feel comfortable, as though I were still at home.

Some TV crews came to film me while I sang, and I learned pretty quickly that the best thing to do when you're being filmed is to pretend that the cameras aren't there.

Then Paul Burger came down from London to make sure everything was all right. He already got on really well with Mum.

The songs I chose for my first album were mostly ones that Lulu had taught me. I sang "Pie Jesu," "The Lord's Prayer," "Jerusalem," an Irish song that's a favorite of Lulu's called "Danny Boy," and the Welsh song that I sang in assembly in St. Mary's Primary, "Suo Gân."

We all agreed on what I should sing, but I only sang what I liked.

As Lulu says, "Probably about eighty percent of the songs were songs that I'd introduced you to and that you'd learned from me. Other songs you've recorded since on the other albums have been suggested by all sorts of different people: Sony people, Maria, or your nan. We're all very close, and we know what you like.

"What I can say is that all the songs have strong melodies. They're romantic. And the lyric content is suitable for a girl of your age to sing. We couldn't let a twelve-year-old sing about being in the throes of passion and wanting to kill herself, now, could we?"

I think Lulu might have a point.

Lulu remembers the experience of making that first album as being quite stressful because it was a new experience — for all of us.

"It was very demanding because we did it so quickly," she says. "We did it in a week. A lot of the songs you had been singing for years, but even so. We had to get it right, and a week's not long. None of us had cut a CD before. We were learning as we went along, and we didn't know what to expect. No one knew if you would manage it, although of course you did."

My album came out on November 9. It went straight to number one in the classical charts. On November 22 it went in at number four in the national charts — or the pop charts. It went double platinum in five weeks.

I didn't know what platinum meant then, but I soon learned that in the United Kingdom platinum means selling three hundred thousand records. In the United States it means a million records, because obviously there are more people in the United States and more people buy records.

When I got to number one, we had a party. We all went over to Auntie Caroline's house for cake and wine, and all the grownups got a little tipsy and Bampy started singing and the telephone kept ringing and my friends sent me cards and some people sent flowers.

We were all in a state of shock. Then Auntie Caroline told us that she had seen my face on the side of a bus. It was a poster advertising my album. That was a big shock, too.

Paul Burger was, as Mum puts it, "over the moon." Later he told us that he was secretly hoping the album would go platinum. He had never expected it to go double platinum — and so quickly.

He was as thrilled, and surprised, as we were.

21

My Second Album

Now that I've told you about recording my first album, I'm going to go straight on and tell you about recording my second album.

I recorded it a year later in July 1999.

Now, a year might not sound like a long time, but *a lot* happened in that year. I'd had a year's more experience and done loads of performances. Lulu says by the time I got to record my second album, my voice was more experienced and a lot stronger and settled and that I was more technically sound.

Thanks, Lulu.

This time round we came up to London and stayed at Terry's flat and recorded the album in the Air Studio in Hampstead, North London.

Air Studio is an *amazing* place. It used to be a church. It has stained-glass windows and an organ, and when I sing in there, it's almost as though I'm in church. It has the same acoustics and the same sort of aura.

And all sorts of fabulous singers have recorded there: Paul McCartney, Phil Collins, Elton John, Sting, Prince, and lots more.

It's pretty inspiring.

For recording the second album, I didn't wear my bunny slippers, although some days I wore my pajamas. I also took all my favorite cuddly toys to sit by my feet and make me feel relaxed and at home.

When I recorded my third album, all I needed was my mobile phone so that I could text my friends and find out what they were up to. What hasn't changed are the cartons of Ribena I drink to give me energy — and hot tea.

I recorded the second album, which was called *Charlotte Church*, with the London Symphony Orchestra, although, as with the first album, the orchestra recorded the music first and I recorded my songs afterward.

I also used a fantastic harpist, Rhodri Davies. He accompanied me on two of the Irish songs, "She Moved Through the Fair" and "The Last Rose of Summer."

I used to play jokes on him. Once I attached a sticker to his back that read "I Am the Harpist," and he walked around all day without realizing it.

We've worked together so much now that, as Rhodri says, "We've reached a point where we're both listening to each other so we're performing as one. Some singers go off on their own, and then I have to struggle to keep up with them."

Rhodri has traveled with me to New York, Switzerland, Singapore, and Hong Kong and all over Britain.

For the second album, I also needed two language coaches. I had a French coach to help me with songs like "Plaisir d'Amour," and I had an Italian coach for the Italian songs like "O Mio Babbino Caro" and "La Pastorella." I love languages, and my coaches were both really over the top, which made learning with them great fun.

The Italian lady kept pushing me to try singing, *"Son bella pastorella . . ."* with longer emphasis on the first syllables, not the last syllables. I had to sing it again and again and again, until I got it right. It was really hard work, musically as well.

The arias took longer to get right than the songs I recorded for the first album because they are much, much more sophisticated.

As Lulu says, "The second album was harder for you, because with the first album you knew all the songs. The second time round, it was taxing because you had to learn more."

We recorded the album in six and a half days, but it was spread out over two weeks. We took lots of breaks.

The typical day started at about eleven in the morning and went on until five, but we would stop for lunch in the cafeteria so that I could have a bacon sandwich or chicken, my favorite food.

My second album was released on November 16, 1999. We couldn't believe it when it went straight in at number one in the classical charts and number thirteen in the pop charts.

Like Mum says, "We were holding our breath to see what would happen. When you went in at number one again, we were just thrilled."

Not that my life changed . . . too much.

That week I went in at number one, I also had a French test, and Abby and Jo spent the night, and we didn't get any sleep.

A pretty fun week, really.

22

Meet the Press

One of the things I've learned since making records — other than that I hate listening to my own records — is that making the records is actually the easy bit.

What is *really* hard work is promoting them. You're traveling around the world, staying in hotels, getting up at five in the morning to do interviews and photo shoots and TV promotions. Sometimes you're singing, but most of the time you're answering hundreds and hundreds — make that thousands — of questions.

Lucky for me I like traveling, I love singing, and I love talking.

After my first album came out, my life changed.

Now I know I said earlier that it hasn't changed, but that's because I've got used to switching from one bit of my life to the other.

Besides, my whole life hasn't changed — and it didn't change straightaway. Mum didn't give up her job straightaway, nor did Dad. My family life stayed the same. School life stayed the same.

What did change was that I had another side to me, like another personality, and it began taking up quite a lot of time. I became Charlotte Church "the singer" as well as Charlotte the schoolgirl, the best friend, the daughter, the granddaughter, and the person I am when I'm by myself.

I had a job. Part of my job was to go and talk about my record.

But first of all came the showcases.

Showcases are different from concerts. They are for music executives and journalists and TV people to come and listen to an artist. At a showcase you're on show. The record company is there to sell you to all these people, so you've got to be good.

Which is why I bring Lulu with me.

When the first album came out in the U.K., I went off round the world to do four big showcases. I went to New York, Tokyo, Las Vegas, and Rome — and all in a couple of months.

It was amazing — and very hectic — and it was my first experience of traveling.

Before I signed to Sony, I'd only ever been

to Turkey and Spain on holiday. I had *never* been to America, nor had Mum or Dad or Lulu or Auntie Caroline. I'd always thought of America as a different world, like a different planet almost, and that it was too good for me somehow.

I don't know why.

Now I realize that America is the same as anywhere else, only completely different, which is why I love it so much.

But before I tell you about my showcases, I quickly want to tell you how many countries I've been to.

Hang on. How many countries have I been to?

Terry will remember. "Terry, how many countries have I been to?"

"You've been to Brazil . . ."

"They have nice boys in Brazil."

"All right Charl, that's not what we're talking about. You've been to Italy."

"I love Italy. I love their pizza and pasta and their art, and they have so much style and history. . . ."

"Holland."

"Holland is so picturesque and pristine and everybody's so friendly."

"Japan."

"Where because Sony is Japanese we went to meet Mr. Oka, who was very, very nice."

"Canada."

"Oh, Canada is *so* beautiful. We went to Niagara Falls in the middle of winter, and it was completely frozen. I've never seen so much ice. I had on two sweaters, a scarf, two pairs of tights, and two pairs of pants, and I was still cold."

"Singapore."

"Singapore is beautiful and tropical, with lots of blossom everywhere."

"I've got work to do. You can do the rest."

"Thanks, Terry."

Okay — to finish off, I've also been to Israel, Switzerland, Sweden, and Australia. But my first showcase was in Rome.

It was in one of the most beautiful places I'd ever been to — the home of the British ambassador to Rome. It was an eighteenth-century palazzo, or small palace. It had a marble floor and huge chandeliers hanging from ceilings painted with frescoes, or murals.

The showcase took place in the evening, and it was quite warm and really magical. There were fountains in the garden and statues everywhere. I performed in a huge hall. I was introduced by the British ambassador, and then I sang "Pie Jesu" and "Amazing Grace" and two other songs. Afterward I remember being asked by a Japanese journalist if I ever got sick of singing "Pie Jesu."

I've been asked this question a lot, because I sing "Pie Jesu" a lot. And every time I say the same thing, which is that every time I sing "Pie Jesu," I do something slightly different with it. But you wouldn't know it to hear me sing it.

The only way I can think of to describe it is that it's a bit like signing your name. Every time I sign an autograph or an album cover or a photograph, my signature is a little bit different. But only I can tell.

My next showcase was in New York, January 1999.

January in New York is very cold and very wet. It wasn't the best time of year to see New York for the first time, but we were really excited to go there. I remember the police sirens and the yellow cabs and the skyscrapers and the steam rising from holes in the road. Everything seemed larger than life.

We were staying at Le Parker Meridien Hotel, which is next to Central Park, and it's where we always stay when we're in New York. You can get the best hot chocolate in the world there. Very sweet with lots of whipped cream.

My showcase was in a Sony music studio near the hotel.

I wore a red trouser suit, and I know that Mum and Lulu were nervous.

The studio was full of people, press people and technicians and sound people and Sony people and producers. I went on stage with Paul Burger. Paul introduced me. I can't remember what he said, but Mum can.

"What Paul said was, 'Outside her family and friends, no one had heard the name Charlotte Church. So I think it's nothing less than remarkable that in the ten short weeks since this album was released, we've been able to sell in excess of six hundred thousand copies.'

"And then he gave you your first double platinum disk, didn't he?"

Well, it's hanging on the wall in the hallway downstairs, so I guess I remember that.

Then I sang "Pie Jesu" and three other songs from the album, and the next day everyone said how well I'd done because there was a headline in *The New York Times* about me.

Back to Mum.

"What happened was that no one knew if Tommy Mottola, who's the president of Sony Music Entertainment and the man who signed Mariah Carey, was going to make it to hear you sing," says Mum. "He did make it, and in the paper the next day they called you 'Tommy's Angel,' which was really nice."

The other thing that happened at the New York showcase was that I met the talent bookers from the U.S. chat shows, and they booked me to talk on *The Late Show with David Letterman* and *The Tonight Show with Jay Leno* and *The Rosie O'Donnell Show* — which you can read about later on.

Then we went shopping. I was only twelve years old then, and I still liked Game Boy and cuddly toys. So we went to the famous FAO Schwarz on Fifth Avenue, and that's when we met John Vernile for the first time. He took us shopping.

I told you he's a *really* good friend.

The traveling didn't stop there. A month later we flew out to Las Vegas for a music convention. I sang one song and was introduced to all the retailers.

We loved Las Vegas. It was everything we thought it would be — and more. All those bright lights and casinos and buildings in the shapes of guitars and pyramids. Mum says my eyes lit up like a child's in a sweet shop as we drove in from the airport in a long stretch limo.

"I never dreamed I'd go to Las Vegas," says Mum. "It took my breath away, and we were both so excited."

I got so excited, I stood up and put my head through the roof window of the limo like a rock star.

We had lots of fun in our own free time. We went to Siegfried and Roy's circus show with the white Bengali tigers that jump through hoops. We saw the pirate ship and threw money in the fountains.

Then it was time to say good-bye.

A few weeks later we were in Tokyo. I was on Easter holiday, so I had *loads* of free time, although first of all I had to do a showcase. I had fourteen camera crews filming me, but it went down really well and I was booked to go on loads of TV shows.

I fell in love with Japan.

I loved the cartoon characters like Hello Kitty on all the clothes and the notebooks and paper and accessories.

I loved the new computer games that I'd never seen before because they hadn't been released in the United Kingdom.

I loved the Pokémon toys and brought lots back for Elliot.

I loved the restaurants where the chefs chop sushi and fry tempura in front of you. Everything's so crazy and busy, and everywhere we went I was given amazing gifts. I was given cuddly toys and a golden pearl necklace and kimonos and a watch.

Everyone was so polite and so lovely.

And then we went to Japan's Disney World. Lulu came with us. I'll let her tell the story.

"When we went to Japan, I saw how much the Japanese love celebrities. I got to see it firsthand because you *were* the celebrity. When we arrived there were promotions on TV saying who you were and that you were about to arrive in Tokyo, so everyone was already really excited about you coming.

"Then we went to Disney World. There were about three bodyguards pushing everyone away, and because of all this fuss people got excited and started shrieking and taking pictures. Oh, I felt so proud. I'd never known anyone so famous."

I remember the fuss, but not like that. I remember feeling tired because of my jet lag and being escorted by lots of Japanese people everywhere we went. Then we went to visit Mr. Oka, who's the head of Sony, and he let me see his solid gold PlayStation. Not all Sony artists get to meet Mr. Oka, so I know I was very honored.

Then it was time to come home and go back to school, although not for long.

On March 16, 1999, my first album, *Voice of an Angel*, was released in America. It went straight to number twenty-eight in the *Bill-*

board chart, and I became the youngest artist ever to enter the top thirty in the *Bill-board* chart. Stevie Wonder had been a month older than me when he did it.

I was thirteen years old.

23

America
the Beautiful

Even though I'm messing up the order of things here, going forward and backward, it's because it seems easier to tell you about things in terms of importance. How they stick together in my mind.

Sometimes I can remember dates and places and facts as though they happened yesterday. Other times it's all a big blur. America deserves a chapter of its own because it means so much to me, to Mum, and to Dad. We've made really good friends there — people we've met through work who invite us to their homes and to meet their families.

I've sold a lot of records in America, and for that I'm really, really grateful to the American public. My first, second, and third albums have sold more than four and a half million copies, which is kind of hard to believe.

I can *definitely* see myself spending more time in America as I grow up and finish school and maybe pursue an acting career. Acting is something I really want to do.

One of my favorite concerts ever was at the Hollywood Bowl, which I'll tell you about later. There are other cities in America that I've been to and loved — like San Francisco and Minneapolis and Nashville and Atlanta — but when I'm in New York I'm always working, and other cities I've been to, like Chicago, I thought were okay.

Los Angeles is our favorite city. In Los Angeles we have fun. We relax. And best of all, we stay at the Sunset Marquis Hotel, where, as Dad says, "you just never know who you're going to bump into."

Dad likes it because it's a rock 'n' roll hotel. There is a recording studio in the basement, and the bar is always filled with musicians and singers from different bands. He recognizes the old faces, and I recognize the young faces.

And we have our own villa — I have an adjoining room to Mum and Dad's — with a balcony and our own little garden and lots of plants and flowers. And there are two swimming pools, and you can have your meals out there.

We've spotted so many fabulous people when we've been at the Sunset Marquis. We've seen Goldie Hawn and Rhys Ifans, who's Welsh, so we had a great chat with him. And David Schwimmer and Lenny Kravitz and Aidann Quinn and Frasier's dad and Ozzy Osbourne — although I didn't recognize him, Mum did.

I suppose, before I'd been to Los Angeles, that I'd imagined it as a place where everyone goes Rollerblading on the beach in the day and goes to movie premieres at night, and a lot of it is like that.

I remember the first time I saw the "HOLLYWOOD" sign. I couldn't believe it was real.

I remember the first time we drove down streets with palm trees and big white houses with pink roofs and when we went to Mann's Chinese Theatre and saw all the handprints of famous actors and actresses set in the sidewalk outside. It was like being in a movie — extremely unreal.

But now that I've been to Los Angeles so much, I've also learned that it's a city like any other city. It's a place where families live and kids go to school and people get the bus and go to the supermarket — and sometimes it rains.

When we go to Los Angeles we always see

a *really* lovely man, Peter Grosslight, who has become very important in my life. Peter is the senior vice president and worldwide head of music of the William Morris Agency.

We actually met Peter for the first time at the Sony offices in London around Christmastime 1998, before my album came out in America. He was with his wife, Carolyn, who's English, and she's lovely, too. She gives me books to read and is always interested in what I've been doing and where I've been.

Then Peter came to my showcase in New York in March, and I joined the William Morris Agency, which we were all thrilled about.

Peter and Carolyn and their two kids, Sammy and Charlie, live in a house in Bel Air. Bel Air is a gorgeous part of Los Angeles. You can hardly see the houses from the road, although you know that all sorts of famous people live behind those big palm trees and high walls. Peter's family live in a beautiful Hollywood house with a long drive and a verandah and a huge garden that goes down in levels to a gym and a pool that's lit up at night.

The first time we went to Peter's house was when I went to Los Angeles to do *The*

Tonight Show with Jay Leno in May 1998. Peter and Carolyn had a barbecue, and Peter did all the cooking. Mum was very impressed.

Peter's assistant, Jermaine Lathouwers, was there. Mum calls her a kindred spirit. They speak on the phone all the time, and she takes Mum shopping in Los Angeles. I was taken shopping by a sweet girl called Jenny. She's sixteen years old and the daughter of a guy from Sony L.A. We went to the Beverly Hills Mall, and I remember being impressed by the amount of different stores there were. Of course, we ended up in the record store — buying CDs. We discovered that we were into the same music, Destiny's Child and Lauryn Hill, so we chatted about music and what concerts we'd been to.

Peter's kids — like a lot of kids in Los Angeles — get to meet lots of famous people. I suppose for them it isn't a big deal, and I think that's what's great about Los Angeles and why I like it so much.

I mean, of course, being famous brings you all sorts of wonderful opportunities, but at the end of the day you're only left with yourself and the people you love. That's why family and friends are the most important things in life.

But I'm getting away from the story.

Peter is only one of the great people at the William Morris Agency, and everyone who works for them really looks after me. They send me scripts because they know I'm dying to act. My plan for this year or next year is to do a movie.

"You could be a movie star or a Broadway singer, or maybe you'll stick with the classics and become a big opera star," he says. "But you can't plan these things too much, it's whatever you want to be. So just keep working and keep focused on the goals you choose. You've got the talent, and the voice is there. You want to do anything and everything, and you're maturing fast. Whether you turn out to be a great actress remains to be seen, but in the meantime enjoy yourself."

Which is what Terry says and Mum says, and I know it's important to keep hold of even though we *do* talk about the future and we're *always* planning ahead. Even I sometimes forget that I'm only fourteen. If I spent all my time worrying about the future, I'd go crazy.

When we first went to America, I was twelve. It was March 1999, and my first album had just been released. First of all, I did the big showcase in New York in January, and then it was time to go on TV.

I did a lot of TV.

Luckily, I'd done enough TV in the United Kingdom to know, kind of, what to expect. Even so, talk shows in America are a much bigger deal. Bigger audiences, bigger studios, lots of producers and backstage people running around — and really funny talk show hosts.

I think the first bit of American TV I did was *CNN Showbiz Today*.

I don't remember being nervous, because I was so used to answering questions by then. What I do have to say, though, is how embarrassed I get when I watch the video-tapes now.

For example, this is the CNN tape.

"Charlotte says she has no plans to cross over into pop."

That's not true anymore.

"However, she would like to match her classical voice with rap artists such as Wyclef Jean and Will Smith. She gave CNN a demonstration of her rapping. . . ."

Agh.

I can't watch any more of that. It's far too embarrassing. Now I'm watching myself on a show called *Fox and Friends*.

"We've all got kids, right? Now, you folks out there think you know what twelve-year-

olds are like, right? Well, I'm about to introduce you to one who's already in the
Guinness Book of Records, and it's not for
stuffing the most golf balls in her mouth. . . ."

Charming.

"When most kids open their mouths, they
sound like this. . . ."

Oh, that's Alicia Silverstone in *Clueless.*

"Then there's Charlotte Church, who
does not sound like your average twelve-
year-old. . . ."

And here I am singing "Pie Jesu."

"*Voice of an Angel* describes her, and it's
the name of her new CD, which has made
her bigger than Ringo . . ."

Ringo?

". . . in England, her homeland. The little
lady with the old lady's voice . . ."

Old lady's voice?

". . . has already performed for the Pope
and for the Prince. . . ."

You get the idea.

After this, the first American talk show I
did was The *Rosie O'Donnell Show.* She's
earthy and funny and makes you feel totally
relaxed.

I sang "Pie Jesu."

"Honey bunny, I can't believe that was
you," she said when I went and sat in the
chair beside her.

"Are you surprised that people think it's you?"

"No, but I think they are."

"Can you do impressions?" she asked.

Now, I don't think I've said this yet, but I'm quite good at doing impressions. My favorites are the New York accent of a Mafia man, a Welsh person obviously, an Irish person, and I do a pretty good Britney Spears and a great Christine Aguilera.

When I went on *The Rosie O'Donnell Show*, my best impression was of Cher.

"Whoa — that's fantastic," she said afterward. "You're adorable." And she gave me my favorite computer game, Game Boy.

That was just the beginning.

I went on to do the *Today* show, *Good Morning America*, *The Donny and Marie Show*, *Entertainment Tonight*. And I answered lots more questions.

Question: "If you could live anywhere in the world, where would it be?"

Answer: "I would love to live in L.A., Wales, and Canada. L.A. has gorgeous beaches, Canada is amazing, so different from over here, the people are lovely and the shopping is amazing. And I love Wales."

Question: "You're in the *Guinness Book of Records* along with a guy who shoots milk out of his eyes. How do you feel about that?"

Answer: "Am I? Oh that's disgusting. Yuck."

Question: "Are you still finding time to do your schoolwork?"

Answer: "Yes. I got straight As in my last exams. I have two private tutors who travel with me, and I have to study for three hours a day."

Question: "Have you got a boyfriend?"

Answer: "No. I go to an all-girls school, and I'm always traveling, so I don't have much free time. . . ."

Question: "And what are the best things and the worst things about being famous?"

Answer: "The best things are traveling and meeting famous people and getting freebies. The worst things are missing my family and my friends and trying to smile when I'm not in a great mood, usually because I'm tired. But if you ask if it's worth it, I'd say yes."

Then I went on *The Late Show with David Letterman*. The first time I went on the show, I remember being a bit surprised by his questions. He's completely different from Jay Leno, whom I love and whose show I've been on five times. Jay is like an old friend now. He's like a cuddly bear, big and warm. David Letterman made me feel a bit nervous, but I've learned it's just his style.

I've been on his show a couple of times, and it gets more fun every time. He's a really funny guy, and he always has me on his show when I have a new album out, which is great.

After doing David Letterman's show, I met my favorite talk show host, Jay Leno.

When I think of Los Angeles, I think of Jay. I mean, it's hard to remember my first impressions of Jay because I've been on his show so many times now and I've been to Los Angeles so many times.

I was so impressed by my very big dressing room with vases of flowers and bowls of sweets and all the lights around the mirror — more lights than I usually get around my mirror, that's for sure. I remember meeting Jay for the first time because it felt as though I had met him a million times before. He's that sort of guy. I was sitting in a chair having my hair and makeup done, and in he came. He's very big, and he has a very big smile and big, sort of square hands.

I was thirteen then and still into Game Boy.

"Hi, Charlotte," he said. "I've got something for you."

And he gave me a Game Boy.

"Thanks."

"And I hear you've got a great voice. I

can't wait to hear it," he said.

Later on on the show I sang "Pie Jesu," and then I went and sat on the sofa he has for his guests. He asked me about Wales and singing for the Pope, and I remember thinking that the show went really fast.

That's the funny thing about TV. You get all pysched up to go on the show, and then when you're on it and you're talking away, it's all over before it's even begun.

"Come back and see us again," he said at the end, which I thought was really nice — and I have.

After the show Jay told me that I reminded him of his mother, who's no longer with us. Her name was Catherine, and she was Scottish.

"I would have loved Catherine to have met you," he said. "So many kids today are brash and noisy and not nice and polite like you. When you live in Hollywood, you meet a lot of show-biz children, and a lot of them are precocious little monsters. It seems like you're enjoying being thirteen, and that's a great thing. You're having fun with it. Life is an adventure, and that's the way it should be. When I was fifteen I was still playing with model cars. Maybe I still am. I have a collection of old cars and motorbikes, and I love every one of them.

"As for your voice, I don't know what to compare it with. It's extraordinary. I'm not a musician, but I do know it's one of the most beautiful voices I have ever heard.

"What is so refreshing is to meet a person who can be ordinary in the nicest sense of the word — and still be exceptional. Your family seems so normal, but they've been blessed with something extraordinary in you."

I told you Jay's a *really* nice guy.

And I went back, like I promised. The next time I went on his show was in May, and by this time my album was out.

"My next guest is the youngest ever performer in history to have a best-selling record on the *Billboard* charts. Tonight she's singing a song my mommy used to sing to me. Welcome to the Welsh singing sensation."

Then I sang "Danny Boy," and Jay loved it.

Jay's been so supportive of my career. He's very important to me.

"Hey, good job, buddy," he said when I sat down next to him. "That was wonderful. You sing almost as good as my mom. I'm crying. It's wonderful."

24

Famous People

Now that I'm telling you about America, what I could do is tell you about my visit to the White House and meeting President Clinton and Hillary Clinton.

But that would be jumping ahead. Before I tell you about meeting the Clintons, I want to tell you about meeting the Pope. Why? Because first of all, I'm Catholic, and the Pope is the head of the Roman Catholic Church. He is the closest to God you can get, and I've always been brought up to believe that he is the most important person I could ever hope to meet.

Not that I'd *ever, ever* imagined meeting him.

When people say I've been blessed, when they're talking about my voice, I don't pay much attention because I live with it and it is part of who I am. But when I met the Pope and felt his hand on my face and saw his pale eyes and heard his voice so close to my face, I *knew* that I'd been blessed.

I'd been nervous about meeting the royal family and the President of the United States, but meeting the Pope was something else.

Afterward I felt so holy and cleansed, and I had such a stupid grin on my face. It was definitely the highlight of my career.

Christmas 1998. I was invited to sing in the Christmas concert at the Vatican. No one in my family had been to the Vatican before, so the invitation to visit the palace where the Pope lives *and* sing for him was like a dream come true.

To me the Vatican is the most beautiful place you could ever imagine. St. Peter's is an amazing cathedral, with marble columns and statues of the Virgin Mary and a huge dome. And in the Sistine Chapel is the Michelangelo fresco the *Creation of Adam*, which I'd always wanted to see, the famous one with God leaning over to touch Adam's finger.

At Christmas the Vatican seemed magical. It was like something from a fairy tale.

I was with Mum and Dad and Nan.

The Italian women in the audience looked fabulous in ball gowns and diamonds. The men were in tuxedoes. I was wearing a floor-length red dress. The stage was white, and I was accompanied by a sixty-piece orchestra. Behind me was a figure of Christ carved out of stone and a *huge* display of roses.

Before I sang, a long procession of women holding candles walked down through the auditorium and onto the stage, where they sang. Then the woman hosting the TV show asked me how I felt to be taking part in the Vatican Christmas show.

"I feel very privileged, honored, and excited," I said. And I did.

I sang two songs. I sang "Hark! The Herald Angels Sing," although I couldn't remember the words and I had to learn them really quickly before I went on.

Then I sang "The Lord's Prayer."

I remember seeing a long row of cardinals in red robes sitting in the front, but I couldn't see much else.

The concert was televised live for Italian TV. Afterward there was a dinner, which was *so* luxurious. The tables were covered with silver and huge vases of flowers. The glasses had pure gold edging. We had nine or ten courses, and we couldn't get through them all.

Sadly, though, the Pope was too ill to be there. But we later found out that he *had* been well enough to watch the concert on

TV and that he had heard me sing.

When I left I was given a papal scroll, which said that I'd sung at the Vatican. It's framed on Nan's wall.

But Nan was gutted not to have met the Pope.

What was meant to happen was that the day *after* the concert, the artists who had performed at the concert, and their families, were to be invited to meet him. That morning just as we were getting ready to go, we had a telephone call telling us that Il Papa, which is Italian for the Pope, was still too unwell. We wouldn't be meeting him.

We were all *really* disappointed, but Nan was sick with disappointment. To come that close to meeting His Holiness and then to have her hopes dashed was *really* upsetting.

Still, even without the Pope being there, she says that my concert was "one of the most amazing nights of my life."

But a month later I *did* meet the Pope. This time I was *really* nervous. And so was Mum, who came with me.

We had to line up in the huge hall where the concert had been held. Different people are invited to meet the Pope for different reasons. I remember there being a lot of brides in line. The Pope was standing up on stage, surrounded by people attending to him.

You know how people are always so much smaller in real life than they are in photographs and on TV? Well, the Pope seemed very old and frail. But he also looked very peaceful and radiant, and he had a smile on his lips. He was wearing a heavy white cloak over a long white robe and a skullcap.

As I approached, one of the people beside him whispered into his ear.

"Ah, *la cantante*," he said to me when I knelt in front of him.

This means, "the little singer."

I smiled, I don't think I said anything, and I kissed the ring on his hand, which I was holding. This was what Nan had told me to do. I had Nan's rosary beads — in fact they were my great-nan's — in my hand, and I was twisting them nervously.

When the Pope saw what I was doing, he touched them and blessed them. Then, just as I was about to get up, he reached out and cupped his hand underneath my chin so that he could see into my eyes.

And as I looked into his eyes, I felt something go deep into my soul. I felt very calm and very warm, as though he had passed something on to me that would stay with me for the whole of my life.

Then Mum knelt down. "I felt too over-awed to kiss his hand," she says. "I meant to, but it all happened so fast. And I just remember feeling so moved that you were the only one he leaned forward and touched."

The Pope made the sign of the cross above Mum's head. When Mum stood up, she had tears in her eyes.

We didn't know what to say, so we said good-bye and then we left. It was incredibly moving, and I was so happy to have Mum there. It was as much her special day as it was mine.

Because my family is Catholic, there has always been more reverence for the Pope than the royal family. Although now that I've met some of the royal family, I feel very honored to have done so. I would also have loved to meet Princess Diana, and I'm sad that I never had the opportunity. But I have met Prince Charles.

October 1998. A gala concert was organized to celebrate Prince Charles's fiftieth birthday. Performers that night included Robbie Williams, Roger Moore, Joan Collins, and Geri Halliwell. The concert was at the Lyceum Theatre in the West End of London, and I remember driving up in the car and seeing hundreds of people standing behind metal barriers, all waiting to catch a glimpse of Prince Charles.

It was a special occasion for me because

Prince Charles is the Prince of Wales. Because of the Welsh connection, we decided that I should sing a Welsh song, so I sang "Men of Harlech."

Rhodri accompanied me on the harp. Then the curtain drew back to reveal the London Welsh Male Voice Choir, who joined me on the chorus. Now at the end of the song I have a top B that I'm always quite nervous about, but it was fine.

After I sang, Robbie Williams sang "Millennium," which was one of my favorite songs.

After the concert, we all lined up to meet Prince Charles.

I was wearing a black, flowery dress. I had Roger Moore, or James Bond, and the comedian Stephen Fry on one side of me and Robbie Williams and Geri Halliwell on the other side. Truthfully I think I was more excited about seeing Robbie Williams and Geri Halliwell than Prince Charles.

I was staring at Robbie. I didn't dare go over and say hello, so he came over and said, "Hi, I'm Robbie," which was really sweet.

"I know," I said.

He's lovely. He's really normal and down-to-earth.

Then Prince Charles arrived.

I remember thinking he seemed warm

and, I know it sounds cheeky, that his ears weren't as big as I thought they'd be. I shook his hand and wished him a happy birthday — Geri Halliwell had just sung "Happy Birthday" for him — and he said, "Well done. You have a lovely voice."

On the wall downstairs in the hallway of our home, Mum and Dad have the photograph of me shaking hands with Prince Charles.

Six months later I met Prince Charles again, and this time the Queen and Prince Philip as well.

May 1999. It was a really special occasion, the official opening of the Welsh National Assembly. I was too young, thirteen, to be conscious of what the event meant politically. And to be honest, my family didn't vote for an independent Welsh government. Even so, I was thrilled to be the only singer asked to take part. And I sang a song in Welsh written by a pupil from a Welsh school who had won a national schools competition.

After the ceremony, I lined up with local dignitaries and the Welsh Members of Parliament to meet the royal family. Prince Charles came first. He was very friendly. He remembered me, which I thought was lovely because he gets to meet an awful lot of people.

"You sang at my fiftieth birthday, didn't you?" he said.

"Yes."

"It was very nice, and I want to thank you again. And today your singing was lovely."

Then he said something really funny.

"You know what you should drink for your voice, don't you?"

"No," I said.

"Port."

I laughed. "Thanks, but I think I'll stick to water. Anyway, you're a prince. You shouldn't be encouraging underage drinking."

He thought this was really funny, and he laughed.

Then the Queen and Prince Philip arrived. The Queen was wearing white gloves. She put out her hand, which I took, and I curtsied.

"Tell me," she said in a very posh voice, "do you sing often?"

I was about to say that yes, I did, although to be honest she didn't seem that interested. It seemed as though she were just being polite.

Then Prince Philip interrupted us.

"Elizabeth, don't you know who this girl is?" he said. "She's got a CD out and everything. We've heard her on classic FM."

The Queen nodded vaguely and said, "Oh yes, I do seem to remember."

She didn't sound very sure.

But I really liked Prince Philip. He's definitely my top royal.

That evening there was a concert for the Welsh National Assembly called Voices of a Nation. It was the highlight of the day. Shirley Bassey sang a song, and so did Bonnie Tyler and Shakin' Stevens.

The best part of the night was meeting Tom Jones. I fell madly in love with him. He sang "Green, Green Grass of Home" and "Delilah" and was so sweet and charming. He lives in Los Angeles, although he has a house in Wales, and I've got some great photos of us together, which Mum enlarged and framed.

We're all huge Tom Jones fans.

I was then invited to meet the Queen again that November at "The Royal Variety Show," a televised performance revue that takes place every year. Comedians and singers and actors perform songs and sketches and excerpts from different musicals like *The Lion King* and *Mamma Mia*.

I sang "O Mio Babbino Caro."

Afterward in the line-up — and I knew what to do this time — I was introduced to the Queen. She was wearing an incredible dress in lots of different colors like a harlequin's outfit. And she must have said something to me, although for the life of me I can't remember what it was.

And I knew this would happen, so as soon as I found Dad I told him what the Queen had said to me. Well, he was so excited, he didn't listen, so neither of us could tell Mum anything.

Mum was furious.

But now, finally, it's time to talk about going to the White House and meeting President and Hillary Clinton. This was another *amazing* honor.

Downstairs on the wall — our Wall of Fame — Mum has the photograph of me shaking President Clinton's hand.

As Dad says, "Going to the White House is the most impressive thing that has *ever* happened to me. It was a great honor. And I couldn't help thinking about all the Americans who must have dreamed of standing where I stood that day."

June 1999. I was invited to sing at a money-raising gala performance in aid of the Ford's Theatre in Washington, D.C. It is the theater where President Lincoln was assassinated, so it's very old. The concert was televised, and the Clintons were there to watch it.

But *before* the concert, there was a tea at the White House, and we were invited. A limo came to fetch us and take us to the White House.

Mum was wearing a crocheted dress. On our way there in the limo, Mum caught one of her false nails in her dress and made a big hole and had to spend all night walking around with a hand in front of her dress.

Mum gets hyperexcited before a big event.

I don't know why, but somehow I manage to take it all in stride. I think it's because if I got as excited as she did, I'd be a wreck and would forget all my songs.

When we got to the White House, I remember thinking that it was smaller than we thought it would be, and I kept thinking about the scene in *Independence Day* where it's blown up and thinking how great it would be if Will Smith came running in to rescue us.

We were shown into a beautiful room with portraits on the wall. It overlooked the Rose Garden.

Then it was time to line up to shake hands with the President. There were lots of actors in the line, although most of them I didn't know. I recognized Nathan Lane from *Mouse Hunt* because it was one of Elliot's favorite films. He used to watch it all the time.

I had no idea who Beau Bridges was, but Mum did.

"Oh, my God, there's Beau Bridges," she said. "Oh, go on, Charl, go over and say hello. I can't because I'm an adult."

Then, as we were looking at him, Beau Bridges came over to us and said, "Sorry to interrupt you, but I just wanted to come over and say hi because we're great fans of your singing."

Mum was dumbstruck.

We thought it was so nice of them, and then they invited us to their house. It's at times like these that I have to pinch myself, occasions when famous people I've seen in the movies or on TV want to talk to me — a schoolgirl from Wales — and even ask me to visit their houses.

That's when the President arrived.

Now the first thing I have to say is that you can see why he was the President of the United States of America. He carries himself so well. He's tall and looks very young, even though his hair is a bit gray, and he has twinkly eyes that make you feel twinkly.

But he does have a big nose. I know it's a bit rude to comment on the size of someone's nose, but you do sort of look round it to see his eyes. But I didn't care about his appearance because he seemed like a really, really nice guy. And he made you feel as though you were the most important person in the room. Mum said the same thing.

He knew all about me, which was a thrill.

"So, Charlotte," he said, "tell me about your singing. How many records have you sold?"

I told him the latest figure, whatever it was at the time, and then I gave him a copy of my *Voice of an Angel* CD.

He looked at the back of the CD at the list of songs. "You're singing my favorite song at the gala tonight," he said. "Did you know that?"

I shook my head.

" 'Amazing Grace.' I just love that song. And you're from Wales?"

"Yes," I said.

"You must talk to Hillary. She's from Wales, too," he said.

Then just as he was about to walk away, he stopped, turned round, and put a hand on my shoulder. "God bless you, Charlotte," he said in his Southern drawl. "God bless you."

"Er . . . thanks," I stuttered.

Thinking about it now, it might have been nice if I'd said, "You too," but at the time I couldn't think of anything to say. He just seemed like such a nice person, so completely genuine and kind, that I was actually tongue-tied, and as I think you've probably realized, losing my voice doesn't happen to me very often.

Then the First Lady appeared. She said hello and told me that she's a quarter Welsh. I know I joked about it afterward and said that she probably tells Polish people that she's a quarter Polish, but I was only being silly.

What she said was that a researcher had found out that her great-grandfather had been a coal miner from the Welsh valleys and that he had come over to America looking for work when the coal mines closed down. And she went into lots more details that I can't remember now.

The funny thing about these sorts of situations is that you're trying to have a normal conversation while at the same time you're thinking, Oh, my God, you're Hillary Clinton and I'm talking to you and I've got to try to remember every single word you say so that I can tell everybody about it later on.

That evening we went to the concert.

I sang "Pie Jesu," and the stunning soprano Kathleen Battle sang "Battle Hymn of the Republic."

But the story doesn't end here.

Later on I learned an important lesson about talking to the press and being careful about my sense of humor. Not everyone gets it.

What happened was that when I went to the ladies' rest room at the White House, I saw a pile of paper napkins stacked next to the washbasins. On the corner of the napkins was the presidential seal.

Now who could resist taking one of those?

I took one of the napkins and put it in my bag to take home as a memento.

A few weeks later I was back in Britain. I was on a TV show, and I was talking about my great day at the White House and the gala concert when I sang "Pie Jesu" and the President's other favorite song, "Amazing Grace."

Then I said that I'd taken a napkin. "I was going to take a tablespoon," I joked, "but it wouldn't fit in my dress."

This was a big mistake. It was the sort of joke I share with my dad because we think it's really funny. The problem was the newspapers didn't think it was funny at all. The next day they had headlines like FALLEN ANGEL and NAUGHTY ANGEL and made it sound as though I were a thief.

Even Mum and Dad weren't amused. They told me in the future to be careful about when to tell jokes — and when not to. I felt very silly, and I learned my lesson: Watch what you say in public.

25

My Best Friends, Abby, Jo, and Kim

I've been so busy flying around the world and talking to you about all the amazing people I've met that I still haven't introduced you *properly* to my best friends, who are totally amazing.

Abby, Jo, and Kim.

The minute I get back to Cardiff, the first thing I do, before I've even unpacked my suitcase or opened my mail, is call them up, and either they come round to my house or I go over to one of their houses.

And like I said, I *really* miss them when I'm away. Although sometimes they come with me.

Jo came to Australia, and Kim came to St. Lucia on holiday with us. I see them as much as I can.

I met them at Howell's. I was friends with Kim first. We just clicked, then she introduced me to all of her gang. Then I met Abby, and through Abby I met all of her friends. We've all got completely different personalities, which is why we get on so well. When we're walking down the street we link arms and everybody has to clear a path to let us through.

First, there's Abby.

Abby is a chatterbox. She has the most hysterical laugh. She sort of jigs around in a circle, but no sound comes out. She has long jet black hair with a purple streak at the front. She has braces on her teeth and blows bubbles with her gum, and she *loves* beads and baubles and glitter. She always wears chokers round her neck and dangly earrings and shawls wrapped round her hips. She's like a butterfly.

When we're in town, she darts around the stores, picking things up and putting them down. She's kind of impulsive.

"I want this. . . . Oh, and I *love* these. . . . And oh, I *have* to have these," she'll say.

Jo is the opposite. Jo is steady. She can be very quiet, or loud when it's just the four of us together, but she's never crazy. She has a great laugh. She squints up her eyes when she laughs. She wears Nike sneakers and baggy pants and her hair, which is blond, in a ponytail. She doesn't wear makeup. She's boyish in a girlish kind of way.

Then there's Kim. Kim is cool. She isn't loud *or* quiet. She looks like a surfer chick. She has long streaky blond hair and wears faded jeans and Hawaiian shirts. She's really creative. She's good at art and drawing and hair and makeup.

My ideal day would be a day out with Abby, Jo, and Kim. I would want the day to go on for as long as possible, so we'd have to get up at seven. Then we'd go and pick up a new Jaguar convertible — the coolest car — and off we'd go to the nearest beauty place. We'd have facials and mud baths and massages until about nine, and then we'd have our hair and makeup done, and then we'd go shopping.

We would each have about £5,000 to spend. We would buy loads of fab new clothes and shoes. After shopping we would go and have lunch until about three — and then we'd go to the amusement arcades until four.

Then we'd go to the gym for half an hour. Maybe.

Then we might go bowling or do a bit more shopping until five-thirty, and then we would go home. We'd have our hair and makeup done again, we would *each* have a hair and makeup person, and then we'd go out on the town. We might go up to London and go to a posh club, and we'd have such a great time.

We would get so many wolf whistles, it would do our heads in. We'd party the night away, and then we would kiss all the boys we liked and go home absolutely buzzing and have a girls night in. We'd do face packs and talk all through the night.

Okay, so when we do get together, it's never *quite* like that.

Really, our favorite thing to do is to meet up on a Saturday and go into town. Abby and I have backpacks, and Kim is talking on her mobile phone, and Jo is walking in front.

We all have mobile phones. Kim's and Jo's mobile phones are dark blue. Abby's mobile phone is baby blue, and it has "21st Century Angel" written on it. Mine is a whole load of colors, pink and blue and lilac, which sort of melt together like a sunset. All of our mobile phones have different rings so that we can tell whose is ringing.

The first shop we're going to is Top Shop, which is *the* best main street store for clothes and bags and jewelry. It's a huge store, and there's a huge screen at the back of the store where they show music videos.

The T-shirts here are really cool. We've found a rack of horoscope T-shirts.

"Where's Pisces?" says Kim. Kim's a Pisces like me.

The logos on the T-shirts are fun: "University of Love," "Little Miss Naughty," "Kitten," "Lolita" . . .

The videoscreen at the back of the store is playing a Britney Spears video.

"I'm into Britney Spears. She's much cooler than Christina Aguilera," says Abby. "She looks cooler, and she loves her fans. Christina thinks she's too cool."

They're both talented.

I'm looking for a pair of denim shorts and a bikini to wear on holiday in St. Lucia. I can't find anything here. "Come on, let's go to H and M," I say.

H&M is another *really* good main street store. I guess the difference is that it's kind of indie, where Top Shop is more teenage.

Abby wants everything. She's got about ten clothes hangers in her hands. "Oh, look at these," she says. She's pointing at a rack of T-shirts with tigers on the front.

"I've already got a tiger top," I tell her.

"What about one of these in cream?" She's pointing to a T-shirt with "ELVIS" written on it.

"That would be lush," I agree. Lush is one of our favorite words.

Fashionwise, at the moment, we're all really into diamanté and studs and ponyskin and flowers and anything Indian. But our tastes change *all* the time.

"Look at these," I say. I've found a pair of really cool sunglasses. They've got big, round black lenses. They're kind of Jackie O.

"Hey, cool, Charl," says Kim.

"Yeah. Cool," says Jo.

Now we're in Miss Selfridges, which is another main street store that's *really* good for accessories. It's a new branch of the store. It's only been open a couple of weeks. They do great imitations of designer clothes like Versace and Louis Vuitton.

Kim has found a pencil skirt with a slit up the side that she's going to try on. Jo has attached a comb with braids of fake hair hanging off it to the back of Abby's hair.

"Ouch," says Abby as her head jerks backward. "It's *really* heavy."

Abby looks hilarious. We're all in hysterics laughing. Abby now has really long dark brown braids. She looks completely different. She looks like a backing singer in an R 'n' B band. She pretends to sing, miming to the music that's playing over the store's sound system.

We can't stop laughing.

"Take it *out*," says Abby. She can't get the

comb out of her hair. "It's hurting me."

Reluctantly Jo removes the comb, and we leave Miss Selfridges. The next stop, before we go to our favorite café, Madison's, is Boots, the drugstore.

Inside the entrance to Boots are loads of perfume tester bottles. We spray each other with so many different perfumes that we can't make out which scent is which. I used to love Estée Lauder's Pleasure. Abby likes Dolce & Gabbana perfumes.

Then we ride the escalator upstairs to the second floor.

"Check your faces," I tell the girls. There is a huge mirrored wall to our left.

"Check your fringes [bangs]," I say.

We all take a look.

Upstairs we head for the corner of the store where the photo booth is, Photo Vision. We gather in front of the mirror on the side of the booth and brush our hair and gloss our lips. I'm wearing a bandanna in my hair. I make sure it's on straight.

Then it's time to cram in.

"Ouch, you're squashing me. Get off," says Jo.

Abby has sat on Jo. I'm not surprised Jo's hurting. I've got my head inside the booth, but my legs jutting out. There's *no way* we can all fit inside.

We put in the three pound coins. Nothing happens.

"What's wrong?" says Kim. "Why hasn't it gone off?"

The flash hasn't gone because someone forgot to press the on button.

"Stupid," says Jo.

I press the button. The light flashes once, twice, three times, four times.

We fall out of the photo booth and collapse into fits of giggles.

"I couldn't breathe in there," says Jo.

Now we have to wait three minutes for the photos to be developed. I get a text message from our friend Naomi.

What are you doing later? TB

I text her back. *We might go to the movies. Do you want to come? TB*

The photographs slide out of the hole at the side of the booth. They're hilarious. Abby has her eyes shut. Kim is pouting. Jo is looking the other way, and I've got my mouth open, screaming with laughter.

"Great pictures," I say. "I'm starving. Let's go."

We make our way out of the store and down to Madison's, which is in the basement of Queen's Arcade, a minimall. We order chocolate brownies and Cokes and lemonades.

Abby is telling us about this really weird dream she had. She always has dreams about cars driving too fast. The really weird thing is, her dad's a car dealer.

"And my dad's a dentist, and I always dream about my teeth falling out," says Kim.

Jo doesn't have weird dreams. "I just have dreams about what I've been doing or who I've seen. If I've been watching the Bachelor Boys on MTV, then I'll dream about them."

"What about you, Charl?" says Abby.

"I hardly ever dream," I say. "I'm normally too tired."

We sit down and talk about stuff.

"School is crap," says Kim.

"We hate it," says Abby.

"But we like all our friends," says Kim. "And we used to be in two different classes, but Abby's going to be in our class next year, which is cool."

"We hate the uniform," says Jo. "We have to wear kilts which are knee length. . . ."

"Although Abby's is knicker length," says Kim.

"And they're *really* hot in the summer," says Jo. "And we have to wear red-and-white-striped shirts."

"And black shoes like men's shoes," says Abby.

What about the clothes other teenagers wear?

"Well, there are the 'moshes,' who wear really baggy pants with chains hanging off them and have skateboards," says Jo. "They're messy."

"Then there are the 'goths,'" says Kim, "who wear black and black makeup and homemade clothes with safety pins, and they're into blood and voodoo."

So what are we?

"We're normal," says Jo.

"Yes," I say.

"Although we're a bit of a mixture because Jo can look a 'bra.' They're the girls who wear side parts and baggy track suits," says Kim.

"And they wear huge gold earrings, six in each ear, like wind chimes," says Jo, "and they wear their hair pulled back really tight, and they've got really strong Welsh accents."

My mobile phone rings. It's Mum. She's sending Dad into town to pick us up. It's almost six o'clock, and she's making tea.

We get up and go.

26

Show Time

Now that you've met my friends, I think you've met all the *really* important people in my life. So I better get on with telling my story.

What happened next?

Well, like Lulu said earlier on, singing live is what it's all about, and I love having an audience. Just as every performance is different and every time I sing my songs they're different, well, every audience is different.

I love the feeling of excitement before I go on stage. I love the uncertainty of not knowing how my singing is going to go, and at the same time the certainty it's going to be okay.

If I was told that I could never sing again, it would be strange having to accept that part of my life — and that side to my character — had gone. Even when I'm just listening to CDs or music on the radio, I always sing along and harmonize. It's difficult to describe how I switch from being the person I am backstage when I'm joking with Dad, who is tickling me and making me scream, to the person I am on stage. I guess it's like shutting your eyes and going to sleep — or opening them in the morning and waking up again.

I just do it.

Some of my favorite concerts have been in America.

My family love coming to my concerts, and I love having my family there when I sing. I feel secure when I'm on stage, knowing that they're in the audience. I feel more on show but less alone, if that makes sense. And I love having them backstage, talking and laughing and telling stories and cracking jokes.

The first concert I did by myself in America was in April last year in Columbus, Ohio. It's a small town and very pretty, and although I didn't get to see much of the place itself, the people were so lovely and warm that I really enjoyed myself. I performed in a beautiful theater, and afterward there was a dinner where we met some of the guests. They made us feel so at home.

That's what we love about Americans.

Last summer I did two concerts in Nashville and Atlanta. Both were special. In Atlanta, when I left the theater I was greeted by hundreds of people lined up outside the stage door to say hi and ask for autographs. I was so overwhelmed. I'd never experienced anything like it before.

One little girl came forward to ask me to sign her autograph book. She had traveled for nine hours to come to the concert. She told me that she had diabetes, then she said how much she liked my earrings. The earrings were diamond and emerald and a gift from a fan, but this little girl was so sweet and lovely, and I felt so sorry about her illness, that I took them off and gave them to her.

I can still picture the look of amazement on her face. I still think about her and wonder how she is, particularly after I sang at the Carousel of Hope concert in Los Angeles, which was to raise money for kids with diabetes.

Another of my absolute favorite concerts is the outdoor concert I do every year in Britain. It's held in Wiltshire in southwest England, and it's called the Wiltshire Festival. The concert stage sits inside what looks like a huge shell. It's big enough to hold the English National Orchestra, which is eighty-four people *and* their instruments. There are marquees where you can buy drinks and sandwiches. There is normally a fire with a roasting pig on a spit. People bring picnics and candles and bottles of wine. There's something very summery and British about it.

If it's a warm night, the candles and the warm breeze and the audience's applause, which sounds like wind, is magical. If it rains, which can happen, everyone just puts up their umbrellas. Not even the weather can spoil it. They still have a nice time.

The first year I sang at the Wiltshire Festival, there were five thousand people in the audience. Last year there were nine thousand people. I love singing there because the audience is such fun. Everybody is very relaxed, which means I feel relaxed. I can sing what I want. There's no snobbery about the type of music people expect to hear.

The conductor is Jay Alexander, and he's very eccentric. He plays all the classical favorites like the theme tunes to *Star Trek* and *Star Wars* and the *1812 Overture*. Last year I sang a duet with Willard White, who is a great baritone, and we sang "You'll Never Walk Alone."

I always have a wonderful time.

But I do have a bodyguard.

The first year I sang at the Wiltshire Festival, I had a bodyguard called Ron. Last year I had a bodyguard called Tony. Both were *really* big guys with a great sense of humor. You need to have a good sense of humor following other people around.

As Andy, the concert promoter and a good family friend, said, "You can't expect to walk around twenty thousand people and *not* have a bodyguard."

Anyway, back to America.

The next concert I *have* to tell you about was in September 1999, which was when I sang at the Hollywood Bowl. The whole family flew out to Los Angeles, Nan and Bampy and Terry and Mum and Dad. They were all there.

The Hollywood Bowl is the *most* amazing place. When I was told I would be performing there, I thought I was going to be singing in a bowling alley. I never dreamed of playing the Hollywood Bowl. It's in the Hollywood Hills, and it has an outdoor stage and seats that go up the side of a hill across from the stage. It seats eighteen thousand people, and they told me that I had a full house almost every night. I did three concerts in a row.

Terry thinks my concerts at the Hollywood Bowl were a landmark in my career.

"To play to that many people and have a standing ovation every night was a triumph," he says.

I had a great time.

First of all, I sang "Pie Jesu." When all the clapping had died down, I could hear Bampy whistling. Bampy's two front teeth are false, and he can push them forward and do the most piercing whistle you've ever heard. I couldn't miss it.

"Shhhh, Granddad, stop whistling," I said.

The audience burst out laughing, and Mum says Bampy's face lit up to hear his name spoken in front of eighteen thousand people.

Then I sang "La Pastorella."

I always try to tell the audience something about each song so that the music means more to them.

"This is about a little shepherd girl who flirts with all the boys, but only has eyes for one," I said. "Not at all like me."

The audience burst out laughing, and I suddenly realized what I'd said.

"I mean, I don't flirt with *any* boys!" I said. The audience laughed even harder.

My conductor was John Mauceri, and he's a lovely man. I went to meet him before the concerts so that we could go through the music. He gave me some very good advice.

"When you thank the audience, because it's such a big crowd, you've got to remember that you can only see the people at the front," he said. "What you forget is that there are a whole load more people at the back. Now some of those people haven't paid much more than a few dollars for their seats, but they're still out there."

At the end of my first concert when I was thanking everyone, I thanked John and I thanked the orchestra, and then I said, "I'd like to give a special thanks to the people at the back. You've been brilliant."

You should have heard the roar that came from the back of the seats. It was amazing. Dad still talks about it.

"It was the first time I'd seen you sing to a live American audience, and you couldn't have asked for a better audience. It was one of the best concerts I've ever been to."

One of the other performances I did in July 1999 was to a much smaller audience, but it was a very special event. I sang at Rupert Murdoch's wedding.

Rupert Murdoch is, as I'm sure you know, the Australian media tycoon who owns a lot of the British newspapers and TV stations. He married a lovely woman called Wendi Deng. The wedding was in June, and it was on his yacht, the *Morning Glory*, which sailed from New York to the Statue of Liberty.

But we were in Los Angeles.

Not that this was a problem for Rupert Murdoch. What he did was send his private jet to come and pick me and Mum up and fly us to New York.

You should have seen his jet — and his yacht. They were incredibly luxurious.

The bathrooms were fitted with gold taps and padded loo seats and bottles of Chanel perfume for anyone to use. There were electronic shutters that went up and down and huge displays of flowers everywhere.

When we got to New York, I had to warm up my voice on the boat. I was wearing a ball gown with a tiny red-and-black dog-tooth print — and no shoes. The boat was antique, you see, so everybody had to take their shoes off. It was hilarious. All these women in exquisite dresses and bare feet.

I sang at the beginning of the wedding ceremony and then later on after the wedding vows. Rupert Murdoch dropped the ring, and everyone was down on their knees searching for it.

I sang "Ave Maria" and "O Mio Babbino Caro" and "Pie Jesu," which, as Mum said, is a funeral song, so it was a bit strange to sing it at a wedding. But it was what they wanted to hear. It was actually Elizabeth Murdoch, Rupert's daughter, who asked for me to sing. I was like a wedding gift from her to her dad.

Afterward we chatted to Rupert and Wendi, who is stunning. Everybody was very, very friendly, and the food was amazing. There was caviar and lobsters and crabs and so much champagne. It was the first time we had been on a luxury yacht and the first time I had seen a view of the Statue of Liberty and the New York skyline at night. I think it made me fall in love with New York a little bit.

When we told Dad about it later, he was really jealous he hadn't been there, too.

27

Rugby Time

When we got back to Cardiff at the end of that year, 1999, two big things happened.

The first thing I did was sing on the Ford millennium advertisement "Just Wave Hello," which was also released as my first single. The second big thing I did was sing at the Rugby World Cup final, which took place in the brand-new Millennium Stadium in Cardiff. I sang "Just Wave Hello" in the closing ceremony before the final game started.

As Mum said earlier, what seems to happen is that my albums are released in November and I don't go to school during November and December because I'm too busy doing press and promotional stuff.

November and December 1999 were crazy.

The Ford commercial went out on November 1. And I wasn't the only one who saw it. It went out to millions of people in ninety-eight countries.

I suppose it was about the whole experience of life. You see a couple arguing, a grandmother dying, best friends crying, a girl running to her father. And it wasn't done in a sickly way. It was beautifully shot. Lots of people said they got a bit teary when they watched it.

The song I sang, "Just Wave Hello," was written by Danny Beckerman. I was filmed singing "Just Wave Hello" down in Cornwall, which is at the end of England. The tip of Cornwall is called Land's End because it's the last bit of land before you reach America.

We filmed in an amazing open-air theater called the Minack Open Air Theatre, which looks like a Grecian amphitheater, although it was built in the seventies. It overlooks the Atlantic Ocean, which off Cornwall is electric blue. It looks like the Mediterranean, not the Atlantic.

We started the shoot at three A.M.

The opening lyrics to the song are "Dawn is rising on a new day . . ." and as I sang, the sun came up. The sky was on fire with pinks and oranges, then a white bird flew through the sky like a dove. I was wearing a white skirt and a white top and a white poncho.

We filmed until twelve the following

morning. I was tired, but in a happy way. It was an amazing experience.

Five days after the Ford advert went out, it was the Rugby World Cup final.

I think the first thing to say here is that the Welsh love their rugby, especially my dad. And I've watched enough games on TV with Dad screaming at the TV set to know, kind of, what's going on.

When Dad still played rugby, sometimes Mum and I used to go and watch him. Until Dad injured his back, rugby was his biggest passion. He used to look forward to his Saturday games even more than going out for a drink.

He played for the Canton Rugby Club. They have their own pitch just outside Cardiff, with a view of the hills, and Dad used to wear black shorts and a blue-striped shirt.

But the problem with rugby is that it's incredibly violent. Dad had his nose broken three times. I can't tell you how many times he came home with black eyes, and then, like I said, he hurt his back.

One time we went to watch Dad play, I remember that he wasn't very impressed with our support. Mum and I were sitting on the touchline. We were meant to be cheering Dad on.

It was the end of the game. Apparently

Dad had just had a very good run and dodged all the opposition. But when he looked over at us, he found Mum asleep and me reading a comic.

Then, just to show how interested I was, I said to Dad, "You never even caught the ball. You were just running after it all the time."

I think that's when Dad tried to explain a bit about what it meant to be a "second-row flanker," that it was his job to set up the ball for the others and pass it back to them. To be honest, I was never interested in the rules.

I remember the Saturday when the front door crashed open and Dad came into the house looking very sorry for himself. He was limping and twisted with pain.

"What happened?" we said, rushing over to help him.

"Training," he said. "The trainer had us sprinting up and down the pitch carrying sandbags. Then, just when I thought I'd survived, and it was all over, my back went. I can hardly walk. I'm in agony."

That's when Dad decided that it would be crazy to go on playing. He was spending more time being injured than he was playing the game. It was no fun at all.

Which was why Dad was really excited about watching the Rugby World Cup final live *and* seeing it in our own Millennium

Stadium. During the final, rugby-mad Cardiff went completely mad.

The big day for me finally came. Although really I should tell the story of singing at the Rugby World Cup final from the beginning, which means the night before.

Mum and I'd had one of our normal last minute panics.

"What am I going to wear?" I said. I mean, what *do* you wear to the opening ceremony of a rugby final?

"It's informal," said Mum. "You don't have to dress up."

In the end I decided to wear my three-quarter-length jeans with gems round the bottom, my favorite black T-shirt with "FEVER" on in diamanté, and the red jacket that I wore on the cover of my second album. Paul gave me the idea of wearing the red jacket.

I laid out the clothes the night before in the guest bedroom. The next morning, after breakfast, a car arrived outside my house to take me to the stadium. The minutes were ticking by. I was due to sing at two-thirty, and it was almost one-thirty. I'd done my hair and makeup, but I wasn't dressed.

"Come on, Charl," said Mum. "The car's waiting."

I went upstairs to get dressed. Seconds

later I was standing outside my bedroom, screaming down the stairs. "Mum!!"

"What?" she shouted up the stairs.

"My clothes. I can't find them. Where are they?"

Mum and I both began searching through all my drawers, in my wardrobe, everywhere we could think of.

"I laid them out on the bed in the guest bedroom," I said.

"Oh!" said Mum as she realized what I was saying. "I threw them away."

"You did *what?*"

"I threw them in the dirty laundry."

Then we had a huge argument, as you can imagine.

Mum quickly pulled my crumpled jeans and T-shirt out of the dirty laundry basket and began ironing them.

Then we jumped in the car. I remember seeing hundreds of rugby fans, some of them with their faces painted like their flags on the streets on their way to the stadium. Even though it was November, it was a bright sunny day.

And who was Dad rooting for? Australia, of course.

We got to the stadium, and we were shown to my dressing room underneath the stadium. Now wherever I sing, in my dressing room I am given sweets. Promoters and concert organizers know about my sweet tooth.

In my dressing room, I found a bowl of candies and chocolates waiting for me. Mum and Dad sat down and waited for me as I warmed up my voice and sang a few scales, up and down, up and down. It's a bit like limbering up before a race.

Then it was time to go. I was led by a group of official stewards in navy blazers through a tunnel painted white with the red dragon of Wales on the wall and into the stadium.

The stadium was filled to capacity with seventy-two thousand people, including the British Prime Minister, Tony Blair; the Queen; and the French Prime Minister, Lionel Jospin.

First of all I walked past the dancers, about two hundred of them in brightly colored outfits. Then I walked past the eighteen different flags representing the eighteen different nations competing in the World Cup, fluttering in the wind. Then I walked past the full Welsh choir and the sixty drummers who would be performing after me.

In the middle of the pitch was a small white stage. I climbed onto it.

I couldn't see the Queen, although I knew she was there, but I could see the crowds and hear their roar. The backing track for "Just Wave Hello" started playing, and I began singing live to millions of people worldwide who had tuned in to watch the rugby. I remember feeling proud to be part of Cardiff's big day and to be in the Millennium Stadium.

But I also remember thinking, Great, here I am singing, while all the crowds in the stands are just walking about, chatting away, eating, and drinking. I don't think the crowd was particularly interested in me. They'd come to see the rugby. But it didn't really matter. At the end of my song, I remember saying, "May the best team win," and then I was led off the pitch to watch the game with Mum and Dad. It was the first rugby match I'd ever watched, not counting Dad's games, of course.

And Dad was thrilled when Australia won.

28

Planes, Trains, and Automobiles

How's this for a typical week:

Friday: Fly to Belfast, Ireland, to record *The Late, Late Show*.
Saturday: Fly to London to do a children's morning TV show.
Sunday: Fly to New York.
Wednesday: Appear on Fox News and *Live with Regis and Kathie Lee*.
Thursday: Fly to Los Angeles. Stay at our favorite Sunset Marquis Hotel.
Friday: Appear on *The Tonight Show with Jay Leno*.

I travel a lot, but I've got used to traveling. I have a routine. I make sure I've always got my CD Walkman, that's the most important thing, and loads of CDs, usually my Game Boy because it's still a good way to kill time,

276

my moisturizers because your skin gets so dehydrated on planes, and my makeup because it's fun to mess around with makeup when you're bored.

I like flying. It's a great way to watch loads of movies and catch up on what I've missed at home. Virgin is a great airline because they give you games to play on your miniscreen. And I love the packs they give you with all the goodies, eye masks and perfume and socks.

I love long journeys because sometimes we fly first class so it's really comfy and I'm free to do what I want to do. What I mean is that at home Mum normally goes nuts at me if I don't sleep, and it gets me annoyed. But when we're flying, I'm not under any pressure to sleep. Sometimes you just *can't* sleep on planes. Sometimes I end up staying up all night listening to music and looking out of the windows at sea and sky. I think flying through clouds is one of the most amazing things *ever*.

Then, when we arrive in our hotel room — and I honestly couldn't tell you how many hotel rooms we've stayed in — the first thing I do is look around to see how big it is. If I'm just with Mum, we share a room. If I'm with Mum and Dad, I have an adjoining room.

I'll have a look at the minibar to see what soft drinks there are and if there are any candies. I'll switch on the TV to see if there's the Internet or PlayStation. Then we'll unpack and arrange all our clothes and our shoes and my beauty products and my toiletries. By then it's usually time to go to bed or get in a car and drive to a TV studio.

When the second album came out at the end of 1999, I went to America to do promotional stuff.

I've been on *The Oprah Winfrey Show* three times. I think she's fabulous. Soon Oprah will be showing a clip of our fantastic Christmas party that helped raise money for a charity for underprivileged children. It was so much fun to give out gift bags at the party and perform along with friends like Billy Gilman. I was so excited to be involved in such a great event for such a good cause.

It was also thanks to Oprah that I met someone really special, a painter named Amanda Dunbar. I met Amanda on Oprah's show in September 1999. It was a show about talented kids.

First of all, Oprah asked me some questions about my singing. "What do your friends think about your success?" she asked.

"Oh, they love it. They get free CDs and backstage passes to all the concerts so they can meet the pop stars," I told her. "They just enjoy it for me."

"And the people who don't know you . . . well, it doesn't matter if they're jealous, right?"

"Exactly."

Then I met Amanda.

Like I said, she's a painter. She's about three years older than me, and she paints portraits and landscapes. I don't know much about art, but I know that her pictures are stunning. And I guess a lot of people think the same way — like Oprah and the people who buy her paintings for lots of money.

I met Amanda again on *The Oprah Winfrey Show* in May, 2000. I know it's skipping ahead, but I want to tell you about this show because meeting Amanda turned out to be *so* great for both of us. We really hit it off. We each thought that the other was talented. Amanda says when she paints she feels like she's listening to her angels, and she said that she thought I sing like an angel.

Then she decided to paint my portrait. I told her not to be silly, but she went ahead anyway. That's when we got the idea to sign some of the prints of the portraits and give the proceeds to charity. Amanda said that because we both have angels in our lives, it seemed right to give the money to Oprah's Angel Network.

We were both so proud to be able to

present our check for $100,000 to Oprah on her show. It was a really great moment and a wonderful thing to do, and it made Amanda and me both really happy.

Oh, yes — and it's Amanda's portrait of me that's on the cover of my third album, *Dream a Dream*. We all love it.

Anyway, going back to my first appearance on Oprah's show in September 1999, as soon as I'd finished it, I had to jump on a plane and fly to New York for the MTV Awards.

The MTV Awards were so exciting because I met so many famous pop stars. I was there to present Best Newcomer Award to rapper Eminem. My co-presenter was Wyclef Jean from the Fugees. I had to sing thirty seconds of "La Pastorella," and Wyclef started rapping. He's a really cool guy, and he was really nice to me. He presents TV shows all the time and gave me lots of good advice.

And who else did I meet?

I met Will Smith, whom I adore. He told me he was watching my career closely. I said I was doing the same thing and that I was doing very well.

"Keep going, girl," he said, which I thought was really nice.

Then I met David Bowie.

"My mum is a huge fan of yours," I said.

Then he put his hand under my chin and said, "So cute."

Then I saw the Backstreet Boys and Lauryn Hill and Whitney Houston and Bobby Brown and, well, by then I was so tired I couldn't think straight and we had to rush off to catch our next plane. I didn't want to leave because we were missing the party, but I was booked to sing somewhere else.

Next stop Geneva, Switzerland, for a performance for Pepsi. The concert was in a castle on the banks of Lake Geneva, which is so big that it looks like the sea. The setting was very dramatic. Men blew trumpets when it was time for the guests to come and eat.

I sang "Ave Maria" and "Danny Boy" in candlelight with Rhodri on the harp to accompany me.

The best bit of the evening was when we were introduced to the president of Pepsi. He seemed like a nice guy, so I decided that everyone should do the Pepsi Challenge — to see if they could tell the difference between the soft drinks that were there: Pepsi, Diet Pepsi, and Sprite.

The president of Pepsi looked a bit taken aback, but he couldn't really say no.

I tied a napkin over his eyes and gave him three different drinks. Luckily he got it right.

A month later I was back in America, in New York, for the Thanksgiving parade. Now I know that in America Thanksgiving is one of the most important days of the year because it's about the celebration of family — like Christmas is for us at home. Still, I don't know how I ended up on the Macy's float, moving *really* slowly in horrible traffic down Fifth Avenue in the pouring rain. I was standing between a gold-painted sixty-foot clown and a huge Snoopy wearing a crown, and I had to mime to the music. No one could have heard my voice above the noise of the traffic and the crowds.

It was an occasion that stands out in my mind for two reasons. First of all, I remember thinking how surreal it felt — the crowds, the skyscrapers, the rain, and the noise — and at the same time how despite the bad weather, so many people along the side of the road were shouting my name.

"Sing something, Charlotte! Sing something!" they were shouting.

I was so surprised that they even knew who I was that it made me smile. As all these people started waving at me, I began waving back. And by the time I spotted Mum, who was standing with our friends from Sony New York, I was grinning from ear to ear.

It turned out to be a really fun day.

Even so, after all this traveling, I decided that what I really wanted to do for the millennium was stay at home in Cardiff.

I'd had so many amazing invitations. I'd been invited to sing for the Pope at the Vatican, where Placido Domingo would also be singing, and for the Queen at the Millennium Dome in London. But my grandparents — the people who mean more to me than any famous figure ever could — wanted me back home in Cardiff, and I realized that was where I wanted to be. For a change, I was going to watch someone else perform. I was going to go see the Manic Street Preachers, whom I adore.

In fact, I don't think I was any different from most people when I decided that what I really wanted to do for the millennium was stay at home. After all the anticipation and the hype, all anyone wanted to do was be with their families and not flying around the world on airplanes that might drop out of the skies.

I didn't like the sound of the millennium bug.

But I was really curious to see London's Millennium Dome, which looks like a giant igloo. I was given the chance when I was invited to sing "Just Wave Hello" at the opening of the "Journey Zone," which is sponsored by Ford.

The dome is in Greenwich in South London, and it's right next to the Thames. Inside the dome are lots of different zones like the "Body Zone" and the "History Zone," with different themes for different exhibitions.

I took Kim and Abby.

I sang at the top of a flight of stairs. People from the press were at the bottom of the stairs. Afterward we were shown around the dome. It looked really interesting, but you need a whole day to see everything. We didn't have time.

It was a *really* busy Christmas. On Christmas Eve we drove back up to London for a concert at Westminster Abbey as part of a TV special. This was where Princess Diana's funeral service took place. I thought about her when I was there. It made me think about Princes William and Harry and how sorry I am that they are growing up without their mum. I know Mum thinks it would have been wonderful if Princess Diana could have heard me sing — and that she was a very good mother to her sons.

Prince Philip and the Archbishop of Canterbury were there on Christmas Eve to hear me sing. I was singing Christmas carols with the Welsh bass-baritone Bryn Terfel. He was singing in Welsh, and I was singing in English. We were joined by the Westminster Abbey Choir in red robes with white ruffs like the boys' choir at the Cathedral School.

Nan watched it at home on TV. Afterward she said she'd been really moved.

I'd do anything for Nan, even stay at home for New Year's Eve, which is what we did. First of all, we had a big dinner at Nan's house, then we went to Cardiff Castle, where, I told you, they hold concerts in the grounds.

On millennium night, the castle and open-air stage were floodlit, and I sang "Just Wave Hello." Then we went to the Manic Street Preachers concert.

It was an unforgettable night. Everyone was in such a great mood. And there was a live satellite link-up with ABC News in New York, and I spoke to America from Cardiff, which was great.

I said, "Hi, America, from Cardiff. I've just done a couple of songs for everyone to hear, and I'm going to see the Manic Street Preachers, and we've had a fabulous firework display."

Best of all, at the end of it, I didn't have to jump on a plane or sleep in a hotel bed. I went home.

And on the first day of the twenty-first century, I woke up in my *own* bed.

29

Twenty-First-Century Girl

The first year of the twenty-first century was so hectic.

One of the great things that happened was that my first official fan club started up. This has made a huge difference to me and my fans. It means that I can reply to some of the wonderful letters and cards I receive. I really have been told some truly amazing stories.

A letter came from a woman in Texas. The story she shared with me was so moving that I want to share it with you. First of all, she asked if there is a word in English that means "greater than a miracle" because she has a five-year-old daughter who is — or at least was — autistic. The woman said that her daughter couldn't speak. Then after the woman bought *Voice of an Angel*, a miracle — this was her word — happened.

When she played the album to her

daughter, her daughter smiled and hummed and kicked her feet. Then she tried singing some of the words. Finally one day her daughter sang "Pie Jesu," and now she's learning new words in English every day. The woman said that it's as if the music opened a window in her brain and caused her to speak.

I can't believe that someone would write me such a beautiful letter and that my singing could have that much effect on a family. Sometimes these letters are quite overwhelming, and I don't know how to respond other than to say thank you.

It is difficult sometimes to know what to say when people confide in me and tell me that I'm an inspiration. All I've ever done is follow my instincts and my heart and worked hard at what I do. All I can do is tell other people to do the same.

This is how I started my most recent newsletter:

Dear Friend

Thank you for writing to me and asking for more information — and sorry it has taken so long to reply to you.

As you can probably imagine, the past year or two have been incredibly busy for me, and added to that there have been some well-publicised behind-the-scenes matters to deal with over recent weeks. . . .

For a start, it was decided to hand over my Official Fan Club from one organisation to another. The new address is PO Box 153, Stanmore, Middlesex, HA7 2HF, England.

I am now able to tell you everything you need to know about my new plans to keep people like you informed. It is not a paying fan club. For the moment we have set things up to provide you with an occasional news-letter — like this — containing information about my past activity and future plans. . . .

As I grow up and am faced with more and more choices, one of the things I've realized is that even though everybody wants to give advice — and I've had some really helpful advice — I have to work it out for myself.

When I met Celine Dion at Wembley Stadium after her show, she said to me, "Don't sing too much. Save your voice."

When I met Robbie Williams at the Sunset Marquis Hotel, he said, "Congratulations on all your success. Don't let it burn you out. Remember, you can always say no if you want to."

The one thing I've never doubted is that I love what I do.

Last January I went back to school, which made a change, and I really enjoyed it. It was part of the reason I decided to try to spend as much time at school this year as possible.

As soon as February arrived, we were back on the road. The following eight weeks of spring 2000 took us to New York, then Toronto, then Los Angeles, then Japan, then Australia, then Hawaii, with a couple of days of rest, and on to Brazil and Sweden. I was doing showcases and concerts.

There were lots of highlights.

One was in New York, where I shot a commercial for the chain store Target. I've become one of their girls, or figureheads, I guess, along with Julie Andrews and Tina Turner. Can you imagine, Julie Andrews, Tina Turner, and me?

I've also sung at Target conferences. Last summer in Minneapolis I met Tina Turner, who was shooting their Christmas spot. She's sixty-two and looks thirty-two. She's absolutely stunning.

In Toronto I performed in the Royal Ontario Museum, and the showcase went out on the Web the next day.

In Los Angeles I made my first U.S. in-store appearance at the KCET Store of Knowledge at Fashion Island, Newport Beach. It was on a Saturday, and the store was packed.

In Japan I gave a showcase on Valentine's Day in Tokyo, and I was given loads of cards and gifts.

Then we flew to Sydney, Australia. This was one of the real highlights of the tour because we met Bampy's three sisters, who immigrated to Australia thirty years ago, and their families. Bampy was so excited when he found out we were going to Australia and were going to meet his sisters. He's never been to Australia.

We all got along famously and had lots of catching up to do.

The other thing that happened to me when we were in Australia was that I turned fourteen. Birthday time. I was sent so many cards and gifts and e-mails, it was unbelievable.

I was also given a party at Sydney Zoo. All the family came to the showcase and then to the zoo. I think zoos are amazing. Even though the animals are in captivity, they are properly treated. They are centers of research and learning, which is why I find them fascinating. Where else can you stroke a kangaroo and hold a snake and see a wombat?

The next day we flew to Hawaii. I was invited there to sing at a conference being held by Ford for all their top executives. We had three days of pure fun. No work. It was bliss, and great for Mum to have some free time, too.

We visited the location used in the opening shot of *Jurassic Park*. We went on a helicopter ride over cliffs 2,700 feet high. We flew through clouds and saw whales, and lava pouring out of a volcano. We swam with dolphins and looked through telescopes at Jupiter and learned about constellations I'd never heard of before. We were garlanded with flowers and treated like royalty.

In March I went back to school.

In April I flew back to America to perform with the Columbus Symphony Orchestra in Columbus, Ohio, and then to San Francisco for the Heroes for the Planet concert sponsored by Ford.

This concert meant a lot to me because it was for such a great cause — and it was hosted by the actor Haley Joel Osment, who's only twelve and was in the movie *The Sixth Sense*. He's become a good friend. We e-mail each other from round the world, and because we're both in the entertainment industry, while still going to school, we understand each other. It's important to be in touch with people who understand the different parts of your world — and your character.

Haley introduced the concert, which was televised.

"Ladies and gentlemen, kids everywhere, celebrating the heroes for the planet, astounding everyday people who have done amazing things, here's my new friend, Charlotte Church."

The first song I sang was "La Pastorella."

Then Haley said, "So — who are the heroes for the planet? Just look around you. Sixty-five of them are here in the audience, chosen by the editors of *TIME* magazine and Ford Motor Company, and they are extraordinary people who have taken the responsibility for the future of our oceans, our forests, and our precious lands. They have devoted their time, even their lives, to this cause."

Then the sixty-five heroes for the planet stood up, and everyone gave them a huge round of applause. I felt so proud to be part of the concert that was honoring them. Then I sang "She Moves Through the Fair," and, like I said, it's fun to give the audience a bit of an introduction to each song.

"This is a really, really fantastic song," I said. "And it has lots of twiddles. So it's lovely and ornamented."

The next person who spoke was one of the heroes for the planet. His name was Simon

Jackson. He's seventeen years old, and he was honored as a hero for the planet for his work with the spirit bears in British Columbia.

We got on really well, and he invited me to visit him in British Columbia and see the white bears for myself. I'd love to. Well, at this point, what I mean is that I've added British Columbia to the long list of places I want to visit when I get the chance.

Then I sang a Welsh song called "Owls." A tribute to the environment — sweeping scenes of sea and sky and rain forest — was shown on the big screens behind me. It was stunning.

The next song I sang was "O Guide Me, Thou Great Redeemer" with the San Francisco Symphony Chorus.

Now before I flew to San Francisco to sing at the concert, a TV crew came to Cardiff and made a little film about *me*. They played it at the concert, and it's a nice little summary of how I see my life, I suppose.

"If I had to describe myself in three words, I'd say I was moody, bubbly, and unpredictable. My family keep me grounded by making me do housework, so it's no different being famous because life is just normal for me.

"My friends are really important to me

because they keep my feet on the ground and they're a bit of normality when I come home.

"I want to go to university because I do well at school and I have a photographic memory, which is very useful for exams.

"Kids my age do not listen to my music, which is understandable because I don't listen to it. I never listen to myself, and I rarely listen to any other classical music.

"I love reading.

"I used to have this kind of teddy bear, Angel Image, and I do have to remind people sometimes that I am a teenager by mentioning my age.

"Because I've had a career so early, I have to think about things really, really thoroughly. I'm quite a deep thinker. I'm always thinking.

"If I had a personal motto, I think it would be 'Think about things while you're doing them rather than do them and then think about them.' "

After the video, my next song was "The Last Rose of Summer." Before I sang it, Hayley said something really poetic, and it made me think about how important the concert was.

"We've learned that the earth can no longer take care of itself. This next song is a traditional Irish song, and it's called "The Last Rose of Summer." By becoming a hero for the planet in any way you can, we can make sure that even the last rose in summer is renewed by a beautiful spring."

We loved San Francisco.

We said good-bye to America and flew back to Cardiff, and I went back to school because I had to do some studying for my end-of-year exams. Luckily I got straight As — mostly.

Then school broke up for the holidays, but I wasn't on holiday yet. I feel like my life never stops.

First of all, it was time to record my third album.

But before doing that, we went on one of the most memorable trips of the year — and my life. Our trip to Jerusalem. Now even though I was there to work (we were filming *Charlotte at Christmas in the Holy Land*, and I gave two concerts), the visit to the Holy Land was so, so special. Not only did I see people of every religion — Orthodox Jews in big black hats, Muslims pouring out of mosques after finishing prayers, a group of Ethiopian monks who live on a roof — but I learned more about the life and death of Christ than I could ever hope to learn in religious studies at school. It made me think about my faith in a real way.

The Church of the Holy Sepulchre, where Jesus was crucified, was one of the most atmospheric places I'd ever visited. It was spiritual in a way that's hard to describe.

I suppose what I'm trying to say is that I had this feeling of total disbelief that in the tomb in the church is a piece of the slab where Jesus' body was laid.

When we went into the tomb, Mum and I both said a prayer.

To get to the church, we walked down the Via Dolorosa, which is the walk Jesus took on his way to Golgotha. Mum was so moved, she almost cried.

I was awestruck, but also very hot. It was over a hundred degrees Fahrenheit, and I was being followed by a cameraman, a producer, and a director.

The following night I gave an open-air concert. I sang "The Lord's Prayer" and "Pie Jesu" and "Jerusalem." Lulu said that she had never heard my holy songs sound as holy as they did that night.

I also sang in the Dormition Abbey, which is huge with a domed roof and sits on top of Mount Zion. They say the Virgin Mary is buried beneath it. Mum and I couldn't believe it when we heard that.

It was a lot to take in, and even now I have

to remind myself of what we saw.

Then, finally, it was time to come home —
and go straight into the recording studio.

30

Dream a Dream

We recorded my third album at Air Studios in London. We recorded solidly for a week.

The studio looked great. Sony had decked it out with Christmas decorations to get us in the Christmas spirit. It definitely worked. There was a Christmas tree cut from gift wrap pinned to the wall and lots of red and silver tinsel hanging from the beams. There was a miniature Christmas tree and, underneath it, like on Christmas Day, a pile of gifts. Every time I recorded a track, I was allowed to open a gift.

What a great idea.

I ended up with loads of makeup and junk jewelry.

As with the last albums, Lulu and Sian Edwards, the conductor, were both with me in the studio and the same great Sony team were in the control booth. Grace and

Charles and Jeremy.

Mum and Dad were also in there.

Dad was reading a book — he's into science fiction, although I think he was asleep most of the time — and Mum was reading a music trade paper. She reads the *Billboard* charts. She always knows exactly what's going on.

Terry, of course, was on his mobile.

In the studio I'm wearing my army green cargo pants and a yellow T-shirt with "Reebok" on it. I've got my hair in a ponytail so that my headphones don't get caught in my hair, although of course they do.

I'm perched on a stool. In front of me is a music stand with sheets of music on it. Lulu is waving her arms up and down and then from side to side like a crazy disco dancer, which means she wants me to liven things up. Put a bit more energy into what I'm singing, she's saying. I know all of Lulu's gestures. She doesn't have to explain anything.

I start singing, "And every mother's child is going to spy . . ." I can hear that my singing isn't as good as I know it can be, so I stop. I burp.

"It's a bit unstable," I say.

"Like you, then, eh?" says Lulu.

I love Lulu's sense of humor.

I start again. "Merry Christmas to you . . ."

I have to stop singing again.

A tube train rumbles underneath the studio, and a plane flies overhead. If we can hear the sounds of the plane and the train, it means the recording equipment will pick it up. This is one of the best studios, with some of the best equipment, in London.

I sing the line again. Lulu indicates with her finger, by pointing at the floor, that I should drop my voice.

"Great," says Grace over the mike that feeds into the studio. "That had a lot of personality."

Other songs on this album include "Angel Gabriel," "The Little Drummer Boy," "The First Noel," and "Joy to the World."

Next we're doing "Silent Night," which is one of my favorite carols.

Grace says, "Let's start in bar thirty-eight. Okay, we're cueing. . . ."

I take a deep breath, close my eyes, and sing. The four mikes positioned in front of me catch everything.

I stop. "I was crud," I say.

"You need to be spinning on the top when the pizzicato comes in," says Sian.

Lulu gets up and moves over to the shiny black grand piano and bangs out the notes. "Let's try again," she says. "This time I'm going to have faith in you using your brain."

"Don't," I say.

"Just relax," says Grace over the mike. "Remember, it's a casual thing."

"Unfold your arms, you little git," says Lulu.

Lulu's right. I can't breathe properly when I've got my arms wrapped around my chest. I drop my arms by my sides. I reach down for one of the Ribena cartons by my feet and take a sip. I stand up again.

Sometimes it's difficult to keep my concentration. I've got the cords from the headphones wrapped round and round my hand.

Concentrate. I take a deep breath. I start singing. It flows. I can feel it. From the corner of my eye, I can see Sian's hands as she conducts me. This time I get it right.

We've got another track done.

"That was superduper," says Grace.

"Not bad for a fourteen-year-old," says Lulu.

"I'm a genius," I joke.

"Sorry, I forgot," says Lulu.

"And now I get to open another gift."

It's a packet of Tunes. Throat candies. Very useful.

We break for lunch. We move to the studio canteen. I'm sitting on Dad's knee as I wait for my bacon sandwich. Dad is trying to tickle me. Mum goes mad.

"Do *not* make her scream, James," she says.

I move tables and go sit by myself. I text Abby.

What are you up to? Are you sleeping over at Kim's tonight? TB

I hate being out of touch with my friends for too long. I like to feel part of their world even when I'm away. My sandwich arrives. I eat it quickly, and then it's time to go back in the studio.

We start up again. I'm trying to sing "Joy to the World." Lulu is conducting me with a pen in her hand.

"Your intonation is flat," she says. "You're sounding Irish."

"I'm running out of breath," I tell her.

Lulu lifts her hands to indicate that I should do the same with my voice. My concentration is scrambled. I start singing like a cartoon character.

"Is this the chipmunk version?" says Grace over the mike.

We all burst out laughing.

I start again. The orchestral arrangement swells, and so does my heart. This is the joyous bit. I sing it well.

Grace plays it back to me. It's good.

"I'm going to smile," I say, and I do.

Now it's time to sing "Ave Maria." It's a song I love. I clear my throat and tug down my T-shirt. The backing track starts, and Lulu puts her hands together as though at prayer.

This is the last song.

Mum and Dad and Terry have gone. When I've finished recording for the day, I'll climb into the car that's waiting for me and be driven back through London's wet streets to Terry's warm flat.

First of all, I have to get "Ave Maria" just right.

"Psyche yourself up," says Lulu.

I slap my hands against my thighs, then against my cheeks. I feel a rush of adrenaline. I open my arms wide and let the music fill me from head to toe. If I let myself, I can imagine myself on stage with a breeze on my face and ahead of me thousands of faces that I can't see. I can feel the energy of all those people.

I open my eyes and watch Lulu roll her arms and her body and her eyes upward. This means I'm doing okay.

"Beautiful," she says as I finish the final note.

"Awesome," says Grace over the mike.

"Do I get to open another gift?" I ask.

"Sure," says Grace.

It's a choker. I love it. It's a fluffy red feather hanging from a silver hoop. I fasten it round my neck.

"Thanks," I say.

"You're very welcome," says Grace.

By the end of the week, we had finished 99 percent of the album. Just one song to go.

Two weeks later I was back in London in another top recording studio. This time it was the Whitfield Studio in Soho, and I was with a different team of sound engineers and producers, although I did have Lulu. I was there to record a duet.

I wasn't nervous, exactly, more a bit apprehensive. Even though I've sung lots and lots of duets, it was the first duet I'd recorded, and it was with a twelve-year-old country & western singer from Nashville whose name is Billy Gilman.

As soon as I started singing though, all my anxiety disappeared. And Lulu was there to talk me through whatever problems I had. What would I do without her, eh?

Billy, who was very sweet, recorded his part of the song. Then I recorded my part of the song. Then we recorded together so that we got the chemistry you need for a duet.

The title of the duet was "Dream a Dream," which is the name of the third album. It's an arrangement by a man named

Simon Hale of a classical piece by the composer Fauré with words by a lyricist from New York. It's classical with a dreamy, trancy sound and a pop beat. I love it. I think it sounds a bit like Moby.

And, yes, it is a departure from what I normally sing.

What I mean is, it's the closest I've come yet to doing a pop song.

As Terry says, "You've made your name as a soprano. To cross over into any other type of music is taking a big risk."

Still, isn't life about taking risks?

Then I had a look at the framed records on the wall. I couldn't believe how many fantastic female vocalists have recorded at the Whitfield Studio: Madonna, Björk, Annie Lennox, the Spice Girls.

Once again I'd found myself lucky enough to be in a truly inspirational place.

31
Turning Corners

Every time I turn a corner, I find the next one waiting for me. Sometimes I think I must really like corners, because I'm always looking for them.

What I mean is, I'm always thinking — and asking, What's next?

Last year I changed management, recorded a duet, visited all sorts of amazing countries — and got on with growing up.

This year I've spent more time at school studying for my GCSEs. I've also been reading scripts and auditioning for movie roles. What I really want to do is act. I've done two bits of acting so far, and I think I'm crud.

Two years ago I was in an American TV series called *Touched by an Angel*. I played a musical prodigy with the voice of an angel. We filmed in Salt Lake City, Utah, which I thought was a stunning part of America. We went horseback riding in the mountains, and the views were awesome.

It was also a great part for me to play even if I was younger at the time and more inexperienced. It was doing *Touched by an Angel* that really gave me the acting bug.

At the same time, I was also in one episode of a British TV drama called *Heartbeat* about a small village community. It, too, was so embarrassing that I can't even watch it now.

But what I do know is that I can act, which means I know I can do better — and be better — if I try hard enough and have lessons. Acting is definitely one of the next directions I want to take.

I've also been planning the next step to take with my music. It's a big decision to make. All I know is that I love singing.

Mum has faith. "Whether you decide to carry this on or decide to stop next week or next year or in fifty years, you're going to be okay," she says. "Because you're different, you'll stand the test of time."

Dad says I've still got to go through the teenage stage of clubbing and parties, and that's a major concern. Mum says she doesn't worry about all that because she knows I'm sensible. Mum says she knows

I'll be happy. She says that her role is to advise and guide so that I learn from my mistakes.

And what I've learned is that no experience goes to waste. Life is made up of building blocks.

Each block makes way for the next block. Because of this, there is something positive to be gained from everything you do. Just be true to yourself and be prepared to work hard.

Right now all I know is that I want to pass my exams and continue singing and see my friends and family as much as possible.

There's also the charity work I do. I don't want to make a big deal of it, but like I said on Oprah Winfrey's show, when you're as privileged as I am, it's important to give something back.

I like being able to give something back.

I'm a big supporter of the National Society for the Prevention of Cruelty to Children. I've been involved with some of the TV fund-raising events. I was in a photo call with Prime Minister Tony Blair when the public was asked to call in and pledge donations. The event raised hundreds of thousands of pounds.

I'm also committed to helping the new children's hospital in Cardiff, which still needs more money for its completion. At an auction recently, a sweater of mine sold for £1,200. And the dress I wore when I met President Clinton sold for £2,000. I was glad to be able to help.

At the same time, my everyday life — going to school, studying, sleeping over at Abby, Jo, or Kim's, going shopping — is pretty routine. And then something will happen that reminds me that even though I see myself as normal, not everybody does.

I have to tell you a funny story about something that happened yesterday when I went to the bakery with Auntie Caroline. We wanted doughnuts.

"Two doughnuts, please," said Auntie Caroline.

As we stood there, we watched the boy behind the counter put one, two, three, four, five, six doughnuts into the box.

"Just two, actually," said Auntie Caroline, at which point the boy, who was already blushing, dropped the box on the floor and all the doughnuts went everywhere.

As he got down on his hands and knees to pick them up, we heard him whisper very loudly to the other boy working behind the counter, "It's Charlotte Church."

Well, of course, Auntie Caroline and I got a fit of the giggles.

It's difficult to know what to do in situations like this. What I've learned is that the best thing to do is to be friendly — and be myself. There was no reason for the boy to be so flustered — or impressed — that I was there buying doughnuts. But it was sweet that he was. When he finally gave the doughnuts to me, I gave him a smile.

"Thanks very much," I said.

"Charl!"

And that's Mum calling me from downstairs.

Nan and Bampy and Auntie Caroline and Uncle Mark and Elliot are here. It's time for dinner.

But stay in touch and I'll see you *really* soon.

Thanks to Everyone . . .

There are so many amazing people in my life whom I owe so much that it's hard to know where to begin. I couldn't do what I do without the love and support and encouragement of my friends and all the wonderful people I work with. The great thing about what I do is that I get to work with so many talented people. Music is collaborative. It's never about just one person, it's about everyone who's involved in making the music — and getting it right.

Family first.

First of all, I have to thank Mum for believing in me and never pushing me, but always encouraging me to be an individual, to stand up for myself, and to sing. I have to thank Dad for getting me to my final destinations on time and keeping me happy. I have to thank Auntie Caroline for her inspiration and the power of her voice. I have to thank Uncle Mark for putting up with his niece when she's grumpy and tired, and cousin Elliot for always bringing a smile to my face.

Very important, I have to thank Bampy for being a rock 'n' roller and believing in his granddaughter's musical ability — and Nan for being Nan. I love you.

I have to thank Auntie Francis for being so funny and Auntie Margaret for looking after the house when we're away so much and getting my school uniform organized. I also want to say thanks to all the rest of my family: Paul and Susan and Alison and Linda and all my cousins for being the best family a girl could ask for.

Next I have to thank Lulu.

What can I say, Lulu? Thank you for being my inspiration, for finding my voice when I think I've lost it, for making me do it again and again until I've wanted to scream — and for never giving up on me.

My heart also belongs to Terry for believing in me in the early days — and for giving Mum and Dad the support they needed and being with us all the way. Thanks also to Josh.

Now to everyone at Sony, which — like I said — I think of as extra family. First of all,

I have to thank Paul Burger. I couldn't have done it without you, Paul, and you mean the world to me and all my family. Massive thanks to John Vernile — I love you, JV — and thank you for your dedication and love. To my special Welshman in the States, Howard Stringer, and much love and thanks to Tommy Mottola, Mel Ilberman, Peter Gelb, Harry Palmer and Jeb Hart, Stacie and Lalla and Terri. And in the United Kingdom, thanks to Chris Black and Chris Griffin and the two Joannas, Adrian, Gary, Brian, Tristen, Catherine, Dej and Becky and John, and anyone I've missed. Many thanks to Sony Worldwide for helping me obtain undreamed-of success throughout the world.

Thanks, thanks, and more thanks to Grace and Charles and Jeremy and Sian for making three fantastic albums with me. I couldn't have asked for a better team.

Thanks, too, to Mark Melton for your invaluable advice — on everything.

Everyone at William Morris deserves huge thanks for all your hard work and support. You're part of the reason why America means so much to me. I couldn't do what I do in America without you. Thanks in particular to Peter Grosslight and Mel and Julie and Germaine and Joel.

Thanks also to everyone at Brilliant for being so brilliant — especially Nicki. And to Jackie Tyson for doing my makeup so well and teaching me how to do it almost as well.

To Rhodri for his wonderful harp playing and traveling with me round the globe. And to Richard and Catherine for teaching me math and French when I'd much rather be in the swimming pool or shopping. You're a total inspiration — and such fun to travel with.

Loads of love and hugs to all my friends, Abby, Jo, and Kim and all my other friends. You know you're right up there with my family in my thoughts and affections. You're the best.

Finally, thanks to my fans, of course, for listening to my music, and to the readers of this story for being interested in following my journey . . . I couldn't have done it without you.

With my love, Charlotte.

The employees of Thorndike Press hope you have enjoyed this Large Print book. All our Large Print titles are designed for easy reading, and all our books are made to last. Other Thorndike Press Large Print books are available at your library, through selected bookstores, or directly from us.

For information about titles, please call:

(800) 223-1244
(800) 223-6121

To share your comments, please write:

Publisher
Thorndike Press
295 Kennedy Memorial Drive
Waterville, ME 04901